SCRIPTURE JOURNAL

STUDY EDITION

ENGLISH STANDARD VERSION

MARK

CROSSWAY
WHEATON, ILLINOIS — ESV.ORG

ESV® Scripture Journal, Study Edition: Mark

The Holy Bible, English Standard Version® (ESV®)
Copyright © 2001 by Crossway,
a publishing ministry of Good News Publishers
All rights reserved.

ESV Text Edition: 2016

Printed in China
Published by Crossway
Wheaton, Illinois 60187, USA
crossway.org

Crossway is a not-for-profit publishing ministry that exists solely for the purpose of publishing the Good News of the Gospel and the Truth of God's Word, the Bible.

The ESV Bible and related resources are available for free access online and on mobile devices everywhere worldwide at www.ESV.org.

RRDS   34   33   32   31   30   29   28   27   26   25   24   23
14   13   12   11   10   9   8   7   6   5   4   3   2   1

HOW TO USE THIS JOURNAL

How can you dig deeper into God's Word? Understand it better? Apply it well? Keep these fourteen foundational Bible study principles in mind when you read.

1. Start with Prayer

Starting with prayer might seem obvious, but it is incredibly important. On one difficult Bible passage J. C. Ryle wrote, "All portions of Scripture like this ought to be approached with deep humility and earnest prayer for the teaching of the Spirit." That is good advice for approaching tricky texts. But it is also good advice anytime you approach God's holy Word. Such a prayer is traditionally called a prayer of illumination, which typically focuses on asking the Holy Spirit to help you understand and rightly apply the Spirit-inspired Scriptures. For example, you could use or adapt this prayer: "Spirit of God, I know that your inspired Word is a lamp to my feet and a light to my path. Renew my mind to understand these words, soften my heart to love you, and strengthen my will to follow in your ways."

Pray before you read!

2. Stay with Prayer

Let God's Word lead you to pray. For example, after you read Jesus' prayer in Matthew 11:25 ("I thank you, Father, Lord of heaven and earth, that you have hidden these things from the wise and understanding and revealed them to little children"), thank him that he has revealed his "gracious will" (v. 26) to you. Praise him that you, through faith, are a child of God! You might also pray a Bible prayer directly, like the Lord's Prayer. Or write your own prayer based on whatever passage you have just read. For example, after reading Jesus' woes to the scribes and Pharisees in Matthew 23, pray that God would protect you from false teachers, keep you humble, and remind of you what matters most.

Let Scripture guide your prayers.

3. Look Godward

Often when we come to the Bible, our goal is application: "How should we live in light of what we have learned?" This is good, but, before you get there, turn your attention upward—Godward! Ask and answer questions like the following: What does this passage show me about God and his character? What does God do or say, love or hate, in this passage? What motivates God to do what he does?

When you read God's Word, look Godward.

4. Keep Christ as the Center

How would you define the gospel? Take a look at Jesus' summary to his first followers:

> Then he said to them, "These are my words that I spoke to you while I was still with you, that everything written about me in the Law of Moses and the Prophets and the Psalms must be fulfilled." Then he opened their minds to understand the Scriptures, and said to them, "Thus it is written, that the Christ should suffer and on the third day rise from the dead, and that repentance for the forgiveness of sins should be proclaimed in his name to all nations, beginning from Jerusalem. You are witnesses of these things." (Luke 24:44–48)

To Jesus, the gospel is grounded in the Old Testament; witnessed in history; centered on his sufferings, death, and resurrection; and proclaimed to the nations so to require a response: to repent of sin and receive, through faith, the forgiveness of sins.

According to Jesus, the gospel about Jesus is the unifying interpretive center of the Scriptures. So, as you read, always ask this question: How does the section declare, reflect on, or apply the gospel?

5. Look for Biblical-Theological Themes

The Bible is not a disjointed group of sayings and stories that are randomly placed together, but it is a grand story of God's work in the history of salvation. So when you read the New Testament, you must be aware that the story it presents (the Messiah has come!) is building upon the story of the Old Testament (the Messiah will come). Major themes include the kingdom, exodus and exile, priest and temple, and the covenant. These themes, and others like them, develop progressively. They follow a historical trajectory (e.g., God's promise to bless the nations is fulfilled as the church makes disciples of all nations) but also include typological connections (e.g., Jesus is the Passover Lamb, whose shed blood saves us from God's wrath) and ana-logical connections (e.g., Jesus is greater than the temple, because he is the great high priest, who sacrifices himself for sinners, and is the permanent presence of God on earth and in God's people).

Your task in reading (a tricky task at times!) is to consider how these biblical-theological themes might be present in the passage you are reading and, as a result, how they might connect to the gospel of Jesus Christ.

6. Hear the Melodic Line

In music a melodic line is the tune within the tune—that is, a succession of notes that creates a distinctive sound. Those notes are repeated regularly and bring unity to the song. Each book of the Bible has its own unique melodic line, and our task as readers is to find these author-placed notes, understand them, and discover why they are played together. Think of the key notes as key words (see the Glossary in the back if you need help!) and the melodic line as the key themes. For example, a possible melodic line for the Gospel of Mark could be *arise and follow the Son*. The word *Son* is a key word, one that Mark begins with ("The beginning of the gospel of Jesus Christ, the Son of God," Mark 1:1) and that he continues to come back to at strategic points. As we read through this Gospel, we learn that Jesus is the Son of God, the Son of David, and the Son of Man. The theme of Jesus' identity matters to Mark. So too does the theme of discipleship—thus the first part of the suggested melodic line: "Arise and follow." Throughout the pages of this Gospel Jesus calls people to follow him, and he details what that means (e.g., to deny self, to love others). Practically, knowing the melodic line helps us understand each passage better because we under-stand how it relates to the overall theme of a book.

So, as you read, keep an ear to the ground. Hear the melodic line.

7. Trace the Argument

Not every book in the New Testament presents a linear and logical argu-ment, as many of Paul's letters do. But making logical connections between sections of a book, and within paragraphs and sentences, can help you understand the author's message. There are many ways to trace an argument to find the flow of thought. A common suggestion is, first, to isolate the idea or assertion and, second, to notice the conjunctions and prepositions and try to make sense of their relationship with the idea. For example, in Ephesians 5:18–21, after Paul offers a command ("Do not get drunk with wine") and the reason to heed that command ("For that is debauchery"), he introduces the main clause: "But be filled with the Spirit." In the following verse he explains some specific ways to be Spirit-filled and/or to express that the Spirit is at work. Paul introduces four subordinate or supporting clauses:

a. "addressing one another in psalms and hymns and spiritual songs"
b. "singing and making melody to the Lord with your heart"
c. "giving thanks always and for everything to God the Father"
d. "submitting to one another out of reverence for Christ."

Of course, not every sentence or section of Scripture is written in such a logical way, but as we read we should seek to find how an author has crafted his message and should hope to identify and understand how each paragraph relates to the preceding and following ones.

8. Read through the Lens of Love

In his classic work *De Doctrina Christiana* (*On Christian Doctrine*) Augustine said that the goal of biblical interpretation is determined by the church's "rule of faith"; that is, our understanding of Scripture must always be guided by our love for God and neighbor. Put differently, if we think a text is saying something that would keep us from love, then we have the wrong interpretation. Of course, Augustine's direction is based on Jesus' answer to the question "Which is the great commandment in the Law?" (Matt. 22:36), namely,

> You shall love the Lord your God with all your heart and with all your soul and with all your mind. This is the great and first commandment. And a second is like it: You shall love your neighbor as yourself. On these two commandments depend all the Law and the Prophets. (22:37–40)

The whole of the Old Testament ("All the Law and the Prophets")—and, we can add, all the New Testament too (see Paul on love's fulfilling the law in Rom. 13:8–10)—should be read through the lens of love. Of course, the laws of God (not stealing, not committing adultery, and so on) are laws of love—the way we love God and others is through keeping all his laws.

So, let the Lord's lawful love lead!

9. Let Scripture Interpret Scripture

Because we believe that "all Scripture is breathed out by God" (2 Tim. 3:16), we expect that the Bible's recording of historical people and events is accurate, its narrative cohesive, and its theology coherent. One of the great truths rediscovered in the Protestant Reformation was *Scriptura sacra sui ipsius interpres*, which is Latin for "Sacred Scripture is its own interpreter." Scripture interprets Scripture! The principle is that we use explicit or clear sections of Scripture to help us understand a more implicit or less clear section.

As you read the Bible, let the Bible itself help you understand its proper meaning and application.

10. Be Changed by Your Bible Reading
Reading the Bible should change us. Before Paul writes "All Scripture is breathed out by God" in 2 Timothy 3:16, he teaches us that "the sacred writings" can "make [us] wise for salvation through faith in Christ Jesus" (3:15). Put differently, the Bible is designed to give its readers saving faith. That is one of its goals. The other is to train us "in righteousness" and to equip us "for every good work" (3:16, 17). Bible reading should strengthen our faith and equip and encourage us to live out that faith in the church and the world.

Therefore, we should "be doers of the word, and not hearers [or readers!] only" (James 1:22).

11. Think of the Original Readers
It is easy, but wrong, to read the Bible and think that everything an author says to his original audience is meant for you today. Sometimes a text is directly applicable. We should love our neighbors today just as much as Jesus' first followers did then. But other times the author, or a character in the author's narrative, is addressing only his first hearers. For example, when our Lord predicts the destruction of the temple in his Olivet Discourse and then commands "those who are in Judea to flee to the mountains" (Matt. 24:16), he means that the Jewish Christians who live in or near Jerusalem in AD 70 should run for their lives and hide in the hills when the Romans come to town. And the next command ("Let the one who is on the [flat] housetop [common in that time and place] not go down to take what is in his house"; v. 17) has nothing to do with you, your house, and some escape plan!

If we seek to interpret the Bible rightly, our interpretation must be based on the author's (or speaker's) original intention to his original readers. The text cannot mean something to us that it did not first mean to them.

12. Grasp the Genres
A genre is simply a type of literature. Some of the prevalent genres in the Bible include narrative, poetry, epistle, proverb, and visionary writing.

Each genre comes with its own rules of interpretation, which can be overwhelming! But take heart—the more you read the Bible with an eye open for the different genres, the more you will start to see that different books should be read differently. For example, you will come to understand that visionary writing uses images and metaphors as symbols—and thus that the depiction of Jesus in Revelation 1 (with "a sharp two-edged sword" coming from "his mouth," Rev. 1:16) symbolizes something about Jesus as judge. In contrast, Jesus' washing his disciples' feet in John 13 is a literal historical record of an event that happened.

So when you read a passage, consider what genre it is in order to discern what it is emphasizing and how you should apply it to your life.

13. Study the Context

As you read, seek to understand who wrote a book, when it was written, to whom it was written, and why it was written. That is the historical context, and the book introductions will cover such significant details. Also, use the study notes when you need light shed on people, places, and events far removed from our day. For example, when the Gospels talk about "lawyers," they are referencing "experts in the Law of Moses" (the first five books of the Bible). The literary context is important as well. Literary context simply refers to what surrounds a text (what is said or happens in the verses before and after) and where the text is found in the whole of the book. For example, Jesus told the parable of the rich man and Lazarus (Luke 16:19–31), in part, as a rebuke and warning to the Pharisees, who Luke informs us "were lovers of money" and who "ridiculed" Jesus (v. 14) after he taught the parable of the dishonest manager (vv. 1–13), which concludes: "No servant can serve two masters, for either he will hate the one and love the other, or he will be devoted to the one and despise the other. You cannot serve God and money."

In sum, if you know the historical and literary context of the passage, you will have a better understanding of its meaning.

14. Read in Community

The Word of God is for the people of God and is meant to be read, studied, and lived out in community. So, like Israel of old, God's people should gather around God's Word to be instructed by God's appointed leaders. (After "all the people gathered" to hear from "the Book of the Law of Moses that the LORD had commanded Israel" [Neh. 8:1], the Bible was read "clearly" and explained as the scribes "gave the sense, so that the people understood the reading," [8:8].) And, like the early church, we too should devote ourselves to "the apostles' teaching" (what became the New Testament) as we fellowship with each other (see Acts 2:42). So bring your Bible to church and listen and learn from good teachers and preachers. Also bring it to Bible study, share your thoughts, and let others help you discover truths you might have missed.

As you read together, you will grow together!

PREFACE

The Bible

"This Book [is] the most valuable thing that this world affords. Here is Wisdom; this is the royal Law; these are the lively Oracles of God." With these words the Moderator of the Church of Scotland hands a Bible to the new monarch in Britain's coronation service. These words echo the King James Bible translators, who wrote in 1611, "God's sacred Word . . . is that inestimable treasure that excelleth all the riches of the earth." This assessment of the Bible is the motivating force behind the publication of the English Standard Version.

Translation Legacy

The English Standard Version (ESV) stands in the classic mainstream of English Bible translations over the past half-millennium. The fountainhead of that stream was William Tyndale's New Testament of 1526; marking its course were the King James Version of 1611 (KJV), the English Revised Version of 1885 (RV), the American Standard Version of 1901 (ASV), and the Revised Standard Version of 1952 and 1971 (RSV). In that stream, faithfulness to the text and vigorous pursuit of precision were combined with simplicity, beauty, and dignity of expression. Our goal has been to carry forward this legacy for this generation and generations to come.

To this end each word and phrase in the ESV has been carefully weighed against the original Hebrew, Aramaic, and Greek, to ensure the fullest accuracy and clarity and to avoid under-translating or overlooking any nuance of the original text. The words and phrases themselves grow out of the Tyndale–King James legacy, and most recently out of the RSV, with the 1971 RSV text providing the starting point for our work. Archaic language has been brought into line with current usage and significant corrections have been made in the translation of key texts. But throughout, our goal has been to retain the depth of meaning and enduring quality of language that have made their indelible mark on the English-speaking world and have defined the life and doctrine of its church over the last five centuries.

Translation Philosophy

The ESV is an "essentially literal" translation that seeks as far as possible to reproduce the precise wording of the original text and the personal style of each Bible writer. As such, its emphasis is on "word-for-word" correspondence, at the same time taking full account of differences in grammar, syntax, and idiom between current literary English and the original languages. Thus it seeks to be transparent to the original text, letting the reader see as directly as possible the structure and exact force of the original.

In contrast to the ESV, some Bible versions have followed a "thought-for-thought" rather than "word-for-word" translation philosophy, emphasizing "dynamic equivalence" rather than the "essentially literal" meaning of the original. A "thought-for-thought" translation is of necessity more inclined to reflect the interpretive views of the translator and the influences of contemporary culture.

Every translation is at many points a trade-off between literal precision and readability, between "formal equivalence" in expression and "functional equivalence" in communication, and the ESV is no exception. Within this framework we have sought to be "as literal as possible" while maintaining clarity of expression and literary excellence. Therefore, to the extent that plain English permits and the meaning in each case allows, we have sought to use the same English word for important recurring words in the original; and, as far as grammar and syntax allow, we have rendered Old Testament passages cited in the New in ways that show their correspondence. Thus in each of these areas, as well as throughout the Bible as a whole, we have sought to capture all the echoes and overtones of meaning that are so abundantly present in the original texts.

As an essentially literal translation, taking into account grammar and syntax, the ESV thus seeks to carry over every possible nuance of meaning in the original words of Scripture into our own language. As such, the ESV is ideally suited for in-depth study of the Bible. Indeed, with its commitment to literary excellence, the ESV is equally well suited for public reading and preaching, for private reading and reflection, for both academic and devotional study, and for Scripture memorization.

Translation Principles and Style

The ESV also carries forward classic translation principles in its literary style. Accordingly it retains theological terminology—words such as grace, faith, justification, sanctification, redemption, regeneration, reconciliation, propitiation—because of their central importance for Christian doctrine and also because the underlying Greek words were already becoming key words and technical terms among Christians in New Testament times.

The ESV lets the stylistic variety of the biblical writers fully express itself—from the exalted prose that opens Genesis, to the flowing narratives of the historical books, to the rich metaphors and dramatic imagery of the poetic books, to the ringing rhetoric in the prophetic books, to the smooth elegance of Luke, to the profound simplicities of John, and the closely reasoned logic of Paul.

In punctuating, paragraphing, dividing long sentences, and rendering connectives, the ESV follows the path that seems to make the ongoing flow of thought clearest in English. The biblical languages regularly connect sentences by frequent repetition of words such as "and," "but," and "for," in a way that goes beyond the conventions of current literary English. Effective translation, however, requires that these links in the original be reproduced so that the flow of the argument will be transparent to the reader. We have therefore normally translated these connectives, though occasionally we have varied the rendering by using alternatives (such as "also," "however," "now," "so," "then," or "thus") when they better express the linkage in specific instances.

In the area of gender language, the goal of the ESV is to render literally what is in the original. For example, "anyone" replaces "any man" where there is no word corresponding to "man" in the original languages, and "people" rather than "men" is regularly used where the original languages refer to both men and women. But the words "man" and "men" are retained where a male meaning component is part of the original Greek or Hebrew. Likewise, the word "man" has been retained where the original text intends to convey a clear contrast between "God" on the one hand and "man" on the other hand, with "man" being used in the collective sense of the whole human race (see Luke 2:52). Similarly, the English word "brothers" (translating the Greek word *adelphoi*) is retained as an important familial form of address between fellow-Jews and fellow-Christians in the first century. A recurring note is included to indicate that the term "brothers" (*adelphoi*) was often used in Greek to refer to both men and women, and to indicate the specific instances in the text where this is the case. In addition, the English word "sons" (translating the Greek word *huioi*) is retained in specific instances because the underlying Greek term usually includes a male meaning component and it was used as a legal term in the adoption and inheritance laws of first-century Rome. As used by the apostle Paul, this term refers to the status of all Christians, both men and women, who, having been adopted into God's family, now enjoy all the privileges, obligations, and inheritance rights of God's children.

The inclusive use of the generic "he" has also regularly been retained, because this is consistent with similar usage in the original languages and because an essentially literal translation would be impossible without it.

In each case the objective has been transparency to the original text, allowing the reader to understand the original on its own terms rather than in the terms of our present-day Western culture.

The Translation of Specialized Terms

The Greek word *Christos* has been translated consistently as "Christ." Although the term originally meant simply "anointed," among Jews in New Testament times it had specifically come to designate the Messiah, the great Savior that God had promised to raise up. In other New Testament contexts, however, especially among Gentiles, *Christos* ("Christ") was on its way to becoming a proper name. It is important, therefore, to keep the context in mind in understanding the various ways that *Christos* ("Christ") is used in the New Testament. At the same time, in accord with its "essentially literal" translation philosophy, the ESV has retained consistency and concordance in the translation of *Christos* ("Christ") throughout the New Testament.

Second, a particular difficulty is presented when words in biblical Greek refer to ancient practices and institutions that do not correspond directly to those in the modern world. Such is the case in the translation of *doulos*, a term which is often rendered "slave." This term, however, actually covers a range of relationships that requires a range of renderings—"slave," "bondservant," or "servant"—depending on the context. Further, the word "slave" currently carries associations with the often brutal and dehumanizing institution of slavery particularly in nineteenth-century America. For this reason, the ESV translation of the word *doulos* has been undertaken with particular attention to its meaning in each specific context. In New Testament times, a *doulos* is often best described as a "bondservant"—that is, someone in the Roman Empire officially bound under contract to serve his master for seven years (except for those in Caesar's household in Rome who were contracted for fourteen years). When the contract expired, the person was freed, given his wage that had been saved by the master, and officially declared a freedman. The ESV usage thus seeks to express the most fitting nuance of meaning in each context. Where absolute ownership by a master is envisaged (as in Romans 6), "slave" is used; where a more limited form of servitude is in view, "bondservant" is used (as in 1 Corinthians

7:21–24); where the context indicates a wide range of freedom (as in John 4:51), "servant" is preferred. Footnotes are generally provided to identify the Greek and the range of meaning that this term may carry in each case. The issues involved in translating the Greek word *doulos* apply also to the Greek word *sundoulos*, translated in the text as "fellow servant."

Third, it is sometimes suggested that Bible translations should capitalize pronouns referring to deity. It has seemed best not to capitalize deity pronouns in the ESV, however, for the following reasons: first, there is nothing in the original Greek manuscripts that corresponds to such capitalization; second, the practice of capitalizing deity pronouns in English Bible translations is a recent innovation, which began only in the mid-twentieth century; and, third, such capitalization is absent from the KJV Bible and the whole stream of Bible translations that the ESV carries forward.

A fourth specialized term, the word "behold," usually has been retained as the most common translation for the Greek word *idou*, which means something like "Pay careful attention to what follows! This is important!" Other than the word "behold," there is no single word in English that fits well in most contexts. Although "Look!" and "See!" and "Listen!" would be workable in some contexts, in many others these words lack sufficient weight and dignity. Given the principles of "essentially literal" translation, it is important not to leave *idou* completely untranslated and so to lose the intended emphasis in the original language. The older and more formal word "behold" has usually been retained, therefore, as the best available option for conveying the original weight of meaning.

Textual Basis and Resources

The ESV New Testament is based on the Greek text in the 2014 editions of the *Greek New Testament* (5th corrected ed.), published by the United Bible Societies (UBS), and *Novum Testamentum Graece* (28th ed., 2012), edited by Nestle and Aland. In a few difficult cases in the New Testament, the ESV has followed a Greek text different from the text given preference in the UBS/Nestle-Aland 28th edition. Throughout, the translation team has benefited greatly from the massive textual resources that have become readily available recently, from new insights into biblical laws and culture, and from current advances in Greek lexicography and grammatical understanding.

Textual Footnotes

The footnotes that are included in most editions of the ESV are therefore an integral part of the ESV translation, informing the reader of textual variations and difficulties and showing how these have been resolved by the ESV translation team. In addition to this, the footnotes indicate significant alternative readings and occasionally provide an explanation for technical terms or for a difficult reading in the text.

Publishing Team

The ESV publishing team has included more than a hundred people. The fourteen-member Translation Oversight Committee benefited from the work of more than fifty biblical experts serving as Translation Review Scholars and from the comments of the more than fifty members of the Advisory Council, all of which was carried out under the auspices of the Crossway Board of Directors. This hundred-plus-member team shares a common commitment to the truth of God's Word and to historic Christian orthodoxy and is international in scope, including leaders in many denominations.

To God's Honor and Praise

We know that no Bible translation is perfect; but we also know that God uses imperfect and inadequate things to his honor and praise. So to our triune God and to his people we offer what we have done, with our prayers that it may prove useful, with gratitude for much help given, and with ongoing wonder that our God should ever have entrusted to us so momentous a task.

Soli Deo Gloria!—To God alone be the glory!
The Translation Oversight Committee

MARK

Author, Date, and Recipients

The apostle Peter passed on reports of the words and deeds of Jesus to his attendant, John Mark, who wrote this Gospel for the wider church as the record of Peter's apostolic testimony. The book was likely written from Rome during the mid- to late-50s AD (though the mid- or late-60s is also possible). Mark's audience, largely unfamiliar with Jewish customs, needed to become familiar with such customs in order to understand the coming of Jesus as the culmination of God's work with Israel and the entire world, so Mark explains them.

Purpose and Theme

The ultimate purpose and theme of Mark's Gospel is to present and defend Jesus' universal call to discipleship. Mark returns often to this theme, categorizing his main audience as either followers or opponents of Jesus. Mark presents and supports this call to discipleship by narrating the identity and teaching of Jesus. For Mark, discipleship is essentially a relationship with Jesus, not merely following a certain code of conduct. Fellowship with Jesus marks the heart of the disciple's life, and this fellowship includes trusting Jesus, confessing him, observing his conduct, following his teaching, and being shaped by a relationship with him. Discipleship also means being prepared to face the kind of rejection that Jesus faced.

The Gospel in Mark

The Gospel of Mark is presented in a way that demonstrates the fulfillment of Old Testament promises. This is clear right from the start, as Mark begins his account by focusing on the fulfillment of Isaiah 40:3 in John the Baptist, who prepares Israel for the comforting arrival of Yahweh to his people (cf. Mal. 3:1). Yahweh will come to pardon—and to rule over—his people (Isa. 40:1–11).

John the Baptist's preparatory ministry marks the continuation of God's long-standing gracious pursuit of his people (Mark 12:1–6; cf. Heb. 1:1). The origin of this pursuit goes back to God's establishment of his good creation, as he places Adam, Eve, and their offspring in a relationship with himself that is creational (living in God's creation), covenantal (living in light of God's faithfulness and commands), and kingly (living under God's rule and in pursuit of the cultural mandate) (Gen. 1:28; 2:16, 18). After the fall of mankind, God pursues his purposes especially by means of his redemptive call of Abraham as the father of his people. Trust in God's provisions will mark the pattern of progressive redemption, including Israel's exodus from Egyptian slavery (Exodus 13–19) and the giving of the Mosaic law (Exodus 20–23). God's pursuit also takes the shape of temporary mediators (judges and kings).

God keeps his promise alive that he will purify a people for himself (see note on Mark 14:53–65) by establishing and ruling over a holy nation (Israel; see Isa. 40:10–11). That nation repeatedly fails in its calling and experiences the disciplines of division and exile, but God never abandons his people. Centuries after the return from Babylonian exile (cf. Ezra and Nehemiah), John the Baptist announces in the desert—a place of preparation, purification, and testing—the great intervention of Yahweh promised by the prophets. Thus, while Isaiah 40 initially points to Israel's return from exile (Isa. 40:1–2), Mark makes it clear that the prophet was ultimately pointing to the coming of Jesus (Mark 1:1–13).

As Mark continues his account, Yahweh surprisingly "comes in sandals" in Jesus, through whom we ultimately see the divinity the prophets had promised (e.g., 2:5–12; 9:2–13; 12:1–12). Yahweh thus comes in the earthly presence of the eternal Son to begin fulfilling the messianic kingdom expectations of the Old Testament (Isa. 40:10–11). Jesus, the eternal Son of God, initially proclaims the kingdom of God, then later inaugurates it through his death and resurrection. Through these actions that ultimately conquer sin and the effects of the fall, Jesus turns out to be the eternally ruling, messianic King (2 Sam. 7:16).

The ultimate purpose of Mark in the context of God's unfolding redemptive-historical pursuit of his people is to testify to Jesus' summons of grace—that is, his summons to discipleship. Discipleship in Mark represents nothing less than God's ultimate restoration of his universal people to the original creation-design and purpose—namely, to "walk with God" (Gen. 5:22–24) and to be restored as true image-bearers of God (Rom. 8:29; 1 Cor. 15:49; 2 Cor. 3:18; Col. 3:10). This restoration gradually overcomes the marks of the fall, based on Christ's substitutionary atonement, healing, example, and teaching. Jesus' sovereign call to surrendered discipleship redresses Adam's sinful independence and disobedience. Discipleship is not merely a certain code of conduct for the disciples. Being a disciple of Christ means joining the people of God in God's creation, coming under his eternal covenant and kingly rule, and living in dependence on God rather than independence from him. We ultimately see that discipleship in Mark flows from dependence upon the Master's captivating and exemplary person, formative teaching, and atoning work.

In short, the Gospel of Mark shows that Jesus comes as the fulfillment of Old Testament hopes and promises that God would graciously restore his wayward people. Mark's Gospel is just that—*gospel*. It is good news.

Mark and Christian Doctrine

This Gospel instructs its readers in simple yet profound aspects of Jesus' earthly ministry. In doing so it stresses the following themes:

1. *The gospel.* From the first verse and repeatedly thereafter, this Gospel stresses the "good news" or "gospel" (*euangelion*) about Jesus. The Christian faith is rooted in the joyous divine pronouncement that God has done what is necessary for human salvation and cosmic redemption.

2. *Christology.* Mark stresses the humanity of Jesus by mentioning emotions like anger, indignation, pity, surprise, affection, and anguish. The Savior did not hover above humans but shared their lot. Yet he was Lord (12:37), announcing a kingdom (1:15 and over a dozen other passages) that defeats Satan (3:26–27) and liberates those tyrannized by evil: "He commands even the unclean spirits, and they obey him" (1:27; see also 1:34; 9:25). Further, Jesus is the Son of God (1:1; 3:11; 15:39). He is the Christ, the Messiah of OT prophecy, as Peter confesses (8:29) and Jesus attests under oath (14:61–62). He is the Son of Man who receives an eternal kingdom from God, "the Ancient of Days" (14:62; cf. Dan. 7:13–14); he has authority to forgive sins (Mark 2:10), is lord of the Sabbath (2:28), and came to serve others, even by giving his life for them (10:45). Yet he will also one day return victorious in judgment (8:38; 13:26; 14:62).

3. *Christ's work.* The suffering of this Son of Man (8:31; 9:12, 31; 10:33; 14:41) points to the core of his saving work. Some 40 percent of Mark's Gospel narrates the last week of Jesus' life, with the cross as the shocking climax. But this was not the death of an ordinary man: he had stilled the waves and wind (4:39; 6:51), literally walked on water (6:48), healed the

sick (6:56), and raised the dead (5:41). In his transfiguration, Jesus shared divine glory (9:2–8) with authority outshining even Moses (the Law) and Elijah (the Prophets). Therefore, as Jesus knew, his death was not the end (14:28; 16:7). Resurrection to eternal life awaited.

4. *Discipleship*. The doctrine that Mark's Gospel supports is not speculative but applied: Christ came to call disciples, equip them, and send them forth. The Twelve he called symbolized the restoration of Israel. God had not failed in former times, but his remnant among the Jews would expand and form the church through the disciples and their faithful labor. Mark lays a foundation for the discipleship enterprise, a core task of every generation's theological activity.

5. *Evangelism*. Mark's Gospel is a rich resource for evangelism. Many scholars see Mark presenting Jesus in a way that shows he trumps Rome and its vaunted (even worshiped) emperors. If so, Mark's Jesus not only fulfills Jewish expectations for a Savior of the world but calls all subjects of the vast Roman world to faith (2:5; 4:40; 5:34; 10:52; 11:22). "Repent and believe" (1:15) is the key to entering God's eternal and glorious kingdom.

6. *Eschatology*. In Mark 13, Jesus prophesies about events that will happen in the end times. Elsewhere, he promises eternal life for his followers (10:30), but he also warns of eternal judgment (9:42–48). Mark witnesses graphically to this coming ominous event.

Literary Features

Of the four Gospels, Mark is most overtly a "docudrama," consisting of noteworthy "clips" as well as typical or representative events; snatches of speeches or dialogues; and commentary by the narrator. Mark's approach to the biographical data is that of a careful recorder. Mark's Gospel, however, is not a biography in the modern sense, as there is no attempt to describe Jesus physically, treat his family origins, or portray Jesus' inner life. Rather, like other ancient biographies (which were called a *bios* or "life"), Mark's purpose is to speak about the actions and teachings of Jesus that present his ministry and mission. Of course, the book is at the same time an implied proclamation and apologetic work that hints at the redemptive meaning of the events recorded. All of the Gospels are hero stories. Additionally, Mark's Gospel is made up of the usual array of subgenres found in the NT Gospels, including calling stories, recognition stories, witness/testimony stories, encounter stories, conflict or controversy stories, pronouncement stories, miracle stories, parables, discourses and sermons, proverbs or sayings, passion stories, and resurrection stories.

Even though the overall format of Mark's Gospel is narrative, it does not possess a continuous story line but is a collection of discrete units. There are crowd scenes, small-group scenes, public scenes, and private scenes. The resulting book is a collage or mosaic of the life of Jesus. The best way to negotiate this format is to regard oneself as Mark's traveling companion as he assembles his documentary on the life of Christ. The main unifying element in the mosaic is the protagonist, Christ himself.

Mark's Gospel (the shortest of the four) is a fast-paced narrative. Mark tends to include vivid descriptive details, and he prefers Greek verbs that portray an action in process. He often records people's responses to what Jesus did and said. Like all storytellers, Mark selected his material by two criteria: he chose events that were *typical* or representative in the life of Jesus (such as miracles of healing and the telling of parables), and *unique*, once-only events (esp. those connected with the crucifixion and resurrection of Jesus).

Key Themes

1. Jesus seeks to correct messianic expectations and misunderstandings (1:25, 34, 44; 3:12; 4:10–12; 5:18–19, 43; 8:30; 9:9).
2. Jesus is man (3:5; 4:38; 6:6; 7:34; 8:12, 33; 10:14; 11:12; 14:33–42).
3. Jesus is the Son of God (1:11; 3:11; 5:7; 8:38; 9:7; 12:6–8; 13:32; 14:36, 61; 15:39).
4. Jesus is the Son of Man with all power and authority (1:16–34; 2:3–12, 23–28; 3:11; 4:35–41; 6:45–52; 7:1–23; 10:1–12).
5. Jesus as the Son of Man must suffer (8:31; 10:45; 14:21, 36).
6. Jesus is Lord (2:28; 12:35–37; 14:62).
7. Jesus calls his followers to imitate him in humble service, self-denial, and suffering (8:34–38; 9:35–37; 10:35–45).
8. Jesus teaches on the kingdom of God, and implies that God continues to call a people to himself (cf. 1:15; 9:1; 14:25; 15:43).

Outline

I. Introduction (1:1–15)

II. Demonstration of Jesus' Authority (1:16–8:26)
   A. Jesus' early Galilean ministry (1:16–3:12)
   B. Jesus' later Galilean ministry (3:13–6:6)
      1. Calling of the Twelve (3:13–35)
      2. Parables (4:1–34)

The Setting of Mark

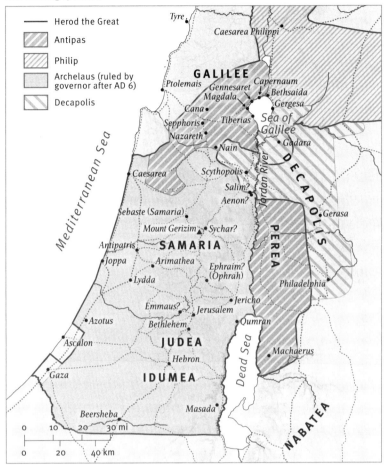

MARK

John the Baptist Prepares the Way

1 The beginning of the gospel of Jesus Christ, the Son of God.[1]

2 [a] As it is written in Isaiah the prophet,[2]

> [b] "Behold, I send my messenger before your face,
>
> who will prepare your way,
>
> **3** [c] the voice of one crying in the wilderness:
>
> 'Prepare[3] the way of the Lord,
>
> make his paths straight,'"

4 John appeared, baptizing in the wilderness and proclaiming a baptism of repentance for the forgiveness of sins. **5** And all the country of Judea and all Jerusalem were going out to him and were being baptized by him in the river

---

[1] Some manuscripts omit *the Son of God* [2] Some manuscripts *in the prophets* [3] Or *crying: Prepare in the wilderness*
[a] For 1:2-8 see parallels Matt. 3:1-12; Luke 3:2-17 [b] Mal. 3:1 [c] Isa. 40:3

1:1–15 Introduction. Mark begins his account with the public ministry of John the Baptist, the forerunner of Jesus.

1:1 Rather than beginning with the genealogy of Jesus (as do Matthew and Luke) or offering a theological background to the gospel (as does John), Mark focuses on the actual **beginning of the gospel** in the life and ministry of Jesus. The "gospel" is the good news of the fulfillment of God's promises.

1:2–3 Mark identifies John the Baptist as the predicted one who prepares **the way of the Lord** (see Isa. 40:3; Mal. 3:1). **Isaiah the prophet** is named because he was more prominent than Malachi, and more of the quoted material comes from him.

1:4 John prepares the way for Jesus by calling people to **repentance**, which means turning to God for **forgiveness of sins**. Baptism was not the means by which sins were forgiven but rather was a sign indicating that one had truly repented. **wilderness.** See Isa. 40:3.

1:5 all the country of Judea and all Jerusalem. John's ministry fulfills the promise of a "new exodus" in which Israel is delivered from the wilderness and symbolically enters into **the river Jordan** again to receive God's promises of end-time salvation.

Jordan, confessing their sins. [6] Now John was clothed with camel's hair and wore a leather belt around his waist and ate locusts and wild honey. [7] And he preached, saying, "After me comes he who is mightier than I, the strap of whose sandals I am not worthy to stoop down and untie. [8] I have baptized you with water, but he will baptize you with the Holy Spirit."

The Baptism of Jesus

[9][a] In those days Jesus came from Nazareth of Galilee and was baptized by John in the Jordan. [10] And when he came up out of the water, immediately he saw the heavens being torn open and the Spirit descending on him like a dove. [11] And a voice came from heaven, "You are my beloved Son;[1] with you I am well pleased."

The Temptation of Jesus

[12] The Spirit immediately drove him out into the wilderness. [13] And he was in the wilderness forty days, being tempted by Satan. And he was with the wild animals, and the angels were ministering to him.

[1] Or my Son, my (or the) Beloved   [a] For 1:9-11 see parallels Matt. 3:13-17; Luke 3:21, 22

1:6 John's clothing and food are like that of other preachers in the desert (see 1 Kings 17:4, 9). **Locusts and wild honey** were (and still are) a source of food for people living in the desert.

1:7-8 The one for whom John is preparing the way (Isa. 40:3; Mal. 3:1) **will baptize . . . with the Holy Spirit** (Isa. 32:15; 44:3; Joel 2:28). John's water baptism will be replaced by the baptism associated with the Messiah. Untying the straps of **sandals** could be the responsibility of a low servant, but it was something that a Jewish person was not supposed to do.

1:9 was baptized. Jesus identifies with the sins of his people, even though he himself is free from sin (10:45). **Galilee** is the region west of the Jordan and the Sea of Galilee and north of Samaria. In the NT era Galilee was ruled by Herod the Great, then by his son Herod Antipas (Matt. 14:1; Mark 6:14), and then by Herod Antipas's nephew Herod Agrippa I.

1:10-11 Mark uses the word **immediately** 41 times in his Gospel. It suggests a sense of urgency and often introduces a new incident or a surprising turn of events. The **Spirit** of God descends upon Jesus at his baptism. Jesus is thus commissioned for a unique service (see Isa. 11:2; 42:1; 61:1). Mark quotes from the OT to show that Jesus is the Son of God (Ps. 2:7) and the servant of God (Isa. 42:1). The heavenly **voice** confirms the eternal sonship of Jesus. All three persons of the Godhead—the Spirit, the Father, and the Son—are involved here.

1:12-13 tempted by Satan. The Greek for "tempted" can also mean "tested." God never tempts anyone to do evil, but he uses circumstances to test a person's character. "Being tempted" indicates that the temptations happened over the 40-day period and were not limited to the three temptations mentioned by Matthew (Matt. 4:1-11) and Luke (Luke 4:1-13).

Jesus Begins His Ministry

[14] Now after John was arrested, Jesus came into Galilee, proclaiming the gospel of God, [15] and saying, "The time is fulfilled, and the kingdom of God is at hand;[1] repent and believe in the gospel."

Jesus Calls the First Disciples

[16] [a] Passing alongside the Sea of Galilee, he saw Simon and Andrew the brother of Simon casting a net into the sea, for they were fishermen. [17] And Jesus said to them, "Follow me, and I will make you become fishers of men."[2] [18] And immediately they left their nets and followed him. [19] And going on a little farther, he saw James the son of Zebedee and John his brother, who were in their boat mending the nets. [20] And immediately he called them, and they left their father Zebedee in the boat with the hired servants and followed him.

Jesus Heals a Man with an Unclean Spirit

[21] [b] And they went into Capernaum, and immediately on the Sabbath he entered the synagogue and was teaching. [22] And they were astonished

[1] Or *the kingdom of God has come near* [2] The Greek word *anthropoi* refers here to both men and women [a] For 1:16-20 see parallel Matt. 4:18-22 [b] For 1:21-28 see parallel Luke 4:31-37

1:14–15 The gospel is the "good news" that **the kingdom of God is at hand**. God's rule over people's hearts and lives is now being established, and people should **repent and believe in the gospel**. The kingdom will ultimately include the restoration of all creation (see Rev. 21:1), but that will come in stages.

1:16–8:26 Demonstration of Jesus' Authority. The first half of Mark's Gospel shows that Jesus has authority over sickness, over the laws of nature, and over the demonic world. It also highlights Jesus' unique and authoritative teaching, and his sending out of his disciples.

1:16–3:12 Jesus' Early Galilean Ministry. The call of the disciples is intertwined with descriptions of Jesus' authority over demons and sickness, as well as with authoritative teaching.

1:20 they left their father . . . with the hired servants. Several of Jesus' first disciples were not poor but were self-employed fishermen. As seen here, James and John were part of a family business. Levi (2:14) was a fairly well-to-do tax collector.

1:22 The main purpose of Jesus' earthly ministry was **teaching** rather than performing miracles or casting out demons, although these actions showed that God was with him. The **scribes** mentioned here may have been a local group of men who taught in the synagogues, rather than the scribes who "came down from Jerusalem" (3:22). Jesus taught with his own divine **authority**, not simply repeating the traditions of others.

at his teaching, for he taught them as one who had authority, and not as

the scribes. [23] And immediately there was in their synagogue a man with

an unclean spirit. And he cried out, [24] "What have you to do with us, Jesus

of Nazareth? Have you come to destroy us? I know who you are—the Holy

One of God." [25] But Jesus rebuked him, saying, "Be silent, and come out

of him!" [26] And the unclean spirit, convulsing him and crying out with

a loud voice, came out of him. [27] And they were all amazed, so that they

questioned among themselves, saying, "What is this? A new teaching with

authority! He commands even the unclean spirits, and they obey him."

[28] And at once his fame spread everywhere throughout all the surrounding

region of Galilee.

Jesus Heals Many

[29] [a] And immediately he[1] left the synagogue and entered the house of

Simon and Andrew, with James and John. [30] Now Simon's mother-in-law lay

ill with a fever, and immediately they told him about her. [31] And he came

and took her by the hand and lifted her up, and the fever left her, and she

began to serve them.

[32] That evening at sundown they brought to him all who were sick or

oppressed by demons. [33] And the whole city was gathered together at the

door. [34] And he healed many who were sick with various diseases, and cast

out many demons. And he would not permit the demons to speak, because

they knew him.

[1] Some manuscripts *they* [a] For 1:29-34 see parallels Matt. 8:14-16; Luke 4:38-41

. . . .

1:23-25 By naming Jesus as **the Holy One of God,** the demon may have been trying to exercise power over Jesus.

1:26-28 they were all amazed. Casting out this demon confirms Jesus' authority to teach.

1:32-34 Sundown marks the end of the Sabbath

Jesus Preaches in Galilee

[35] [a]And rising very early in the morning, while it was still dark, he departed and went out to a desolate place, and there he prayed. [36] And Simon and those who were with him searched for him, [37] and they found him and said to him, "Everyone is looking for you." [38] And he said to them, "Let us go on to the next towns, that I may preach there also, for that is why I came out." [39] And he went throughout all Galilee, preaching in their synagogues and casting out demons.

Jesus Cleanses a Leper

[40] [b]And a leper[1] came to him, imploring him, and kneeling said to him, "If you will, you can make me clean." [41] Moved with pity, he stretched out his hand and touched him and said to him, "I will; be clean." [42] And immediately the leprosy left him, and he was made clean. [43] And Jesus[2] sternly charged him and sent him away at once, [44] and said to him, "See that you say nothing to anyone, but go, show yourself to the priest and offer for your cleansing what Moses commanded, for a proof to them." [45] But he went out and began to talk freely about it, and to spread the news, so that Jesus could no longer openly enter a town, but was out in desolate places, and people were coming to him from every quarter.

---

[1] *Leprosy* was a term for several skin diseases; see Leviticus 13 [2] Greek *he*; also verse 45 [a] For 1:35-38 see parallel Luke 4:42, 43 [b] For 1:40-44 see parallels Matt. 8:2-4; Luke 5:12-14

(roughly 6:00 p.m. Saturday). People are now permitted to come to Jesus with their needs.

1:40 A leper is ceremonially unclean (Lev. 13:45–46). As an outcast, he is financially and socially isolated, and is dependent on charity.

1:41-42 touched him. Instead of the leper making Jesus unclean, Jesus' touch actually makes the leper **clean.**

1:44 say nothing. This is Mark's first report of Jesus telling a healed person not to tell anyone of his being healed. Jesus does not want to draw crowds who come simply for the sake of miracles.. **Show yourself to the priest** is commanded so that the healed person will be declared ceremonially clean (Lev. 14:2-31).

1:45 The people often miss the true purpose of Jesus' ministry by focusing too much on his miracles.

Jesus Heals a Paralytic

2 And when he returned to Capernaum after some days, it was reported that he was at home. ² And many were gathered together, so that there was no more room, not even at the door. And he was preaching the word to them. ³ ᵃ And they came, bringing to him a paralytic carried by four men. ⁴ And when they could not get near him because of the crowd, they removed the roof above him, and when they had made an opening, they let down the bed on which the paralytic lay. ⁵ And when Jesus saw their faith, he said to the paralytic, "Son, your sins are forgiven." ⁶ Now some of the scribes were sitting there, questioning in their hearts, ⁷ "Why does this man speak like that? He is blaspheming! Who can forgive sins but God alone?" ⁸ And immediately Jesus, perceiving in his spirit that they thus questioned within themselves, said to them, "Why do you question these things in your hearts? ⁹ Which is easier, to say to the paralytic, 'Your sins are forgiven,' or to say, 'Rise, take up your bed and walk'? ¹⁰ But that you may know that the Son of Man has authority on earth to forgive sins"—he said to the paralytic— ¹¹ "I say to you, rise, pick up your bed, and go home." ¹² And he rose and immediately picked up his bed and went out before them

ᵃ For 2:3-12 see parallels Matt. 9:2-8; Luke 5:17-26

2:1 Jesus returns to **Capernaum** (c. 20 miles [32 km] northeast of Nazareth), which serves as the base for his Galilean ministry.

2:2 no more room. The house probably held no more than 50 people.

2:4 The flat **roof** consisted of branches or sticks combined with clay. It could be accessed from the outside.

2:5-7 Their faith probably refers to the faith of the friends who brought the paralytic to Jesus, but it may include the faith of the paralytic as well. **your sins are forgiven.** Jesus claims to be able to forgive sins, as **God alone** can. Therefore his opponents think that he is guilty of blasphemy, which is

punishable by death (Lev. 24:10–23; Num. 15:30–31; Mark 14:62–64).

2:8 perceiving . . . that they thus questioned within themselves. As God, Jesus could know things that only God knows.

2:9–11 Which is easier? The fact that Jesus can do the visible miracle (heal the paralytic) is evidence that he can also do the more difficult invisible miracle (forgive sins).

2:10 The healing of the **paralytic** verifies that Jesus also has divine **authority . . . to forgive sins. Son of Man** is the way Jesus most frequently refers to himself in Mark's Gospel. The term refers to both his human and his divine natures. See 8:38; 13:26; cf. Dan. 7:13–14.

all, so that they were all amazed and glorified God, saying, "We never saw anything like this!"

Jesus Calls Levi

[13] He went out again beside the sea, and all the crowd was coming to him, and he was teaching them. [14] [a]And as he passed by, he saw Levi the son of Alphaeus sitting at the tax booth, and he said to him, "Follow me." And he rose and followed him.

[15] And as he reclined at table in his house, many tax collectors and sinners were reclining with Jesus and his disciples, for there were many who followed him. [16] And the scribes of [1] the Pharisees, when they saw that he was eating with sinners and tax collectors, said to his disciples, "Why does he eat [2] with tax collectors and sinners?" [17] And when Jesus heard it, he said to them, "Those who are well have no need of a physician, but those who are sick. I came not to call the righteous, but sinners."

A Question About Fasting

[18] Now John's disciples and the Pharisees were fasting. And people came and said to him, "Why do John's disciples and the disciples of the Pharisees fast, but your disciples do not fast?" [19] And Jesus said to them, "Can the wedding

---

[1] Some manuscripts *and* [2] Some manuscripts add *and drink* [a] For 2:14-22 see parallels Matt. 9:9-17; Luke 5:27-39

2:14 Jesus continues to focus on "teaching" (v. 13; see note on 1:14–15). **Levi** (also called "Matthew"; 3:18; Matt. 9:9) collected taxes and thus was despised for collaborating with the Roman Empire. Most tax collectors kept some of the tax money for themselves. "Beside the sea" (Mark 2:13) suggests that the **tax booth** was by the Sea of Galilee and was used for taxing fishermen.

2:15–16 To recline **at table** indicates personal friendship. When dining formally in a home, guests reclined on a couch that stretched around three sides of a room. The guests' heads were toward the tables and their feet toward the wall. **tax collectors and sinners**. According to the **Pharisees**, Jesus should keep himself "clean" from such people (see Lev. 10:10).

2:17 Jesus compares those who are **well** to those who are **righteous**, and those who are **sick** to **sinners**.

2:18 fasting. Various kinds of fasts were practiced in OT times, though the law required only one fast a year, on the Day of Atonement.

2:19–20 Jesus refers to himself as **the bridegroom**. In the OT, God the Father was the bridegroom (see Isa. 62:5; Hos. 2:19–20). **then they will fast**. When Jesus is taken away from his disciples (when he dies), they will return to fasting in order to seek

guests fast while the bridegroom is with them? As long as they have the bridegroom with them, they cannot fast. [20] The days will come when the bridegroom is taken away from them, and then they will fast in that day. [21] No one sews a piece of unshrunk cloth on an old garment. If he does, the patch tears away from it, the new from the old, and a worse tear is made. [22] And no one puts new wine into old wineskins. If he does, the wine will burst the skins—and the wine is destroyed, and so are the skins. But new wine is for fresh wineskins."[1]

Jesus Is Lord of the Sabbath

[23] [a] One Sabbath he was going through the grainfields, and as they made their way, his disciples began to pluck heads of grain. [24] And the Pharisees were saying to him, "Look, why are they doing what is not lawful on the Sabbath?" [25] And he said to them, "Have you never read what David did, when he was in need and was hungry, he and those who were with him: [26] how he entered the house of God, in the time of[2] Abiathar the high priest, and ate the bread of the Presence, which it is not lawful for any but the priests to eat, and also gave it to those who were with him?" [27] And he said to them, "The Sabbath was made for man, not man for the Sabbath. [28] So the Son of Man is lord even of the Sabbath."

[1] Some manuscripts omit *But new wine is for fresh wineskins* [2] Or *in the passage about* [a] For 2:23-28 see parallels Matt. 12:1-8; Luke 6:1-5

God's presence. But they do not need to do that when he is still with them (see Isa. 53:8).

2:21–22 unshrunk cloth . . . old garment. . . . new wine . . . old wineskins. The kingdom of God is not merely a patch over the Mosaic law and Jewish traditions. Jesus brings a new era, with new ways.

2:23–24 Deuteronomy 23:25 implies that, if a person is hungry, he is permitted to eat **heads of grain** from any field he might pass by. However the Pharisees decreed that, since plucking the grain involves "work," it could not be done on the **Sabbath**.

2:25–26 The fact that David ate the **bread of the Presence** (1 Sam. 21:1–6) means that, if there is a serious need, actions are allowed on a Sabbath that otherwise might not be permitted.

2:27–28 Son of Man (see Dan. 7:13) is Jesus' favorite of describing himself. It shows the true meaning of his identity and ministry: (1) the humble servant who has come to forgive common sinners; (2) the suffering servant whose atoning death and resurrection will redeem his people; and (3) the glorious King and Judge who will return to establish God's kingdom on earth. If the Sabbath is for the benefit of mankind, and if the Son of Man is Lord over all mankind, then the Son of Man is surely **lord even of the Sabbath**.

A Man with a Withered Hand

3 [a]Again he entered the synagogue, and a man was there with a withered hand. [2]And they watched Jesus,[1] to see whether he would heal him on the Sabbath, so that they might accuse him. [3]And he said to the man with the withered hand, "Come here." [4]And he said to them, "Is it lawful on the Sabbath to do good or to do harm, to save life or to kill?" But they were silent. [5]And he looked around at them with anger, grieved at their hardness of heart, and said to the man, "Stretch out your hand." He stretched it out, and his hand was restored. [6]The Pharisees went out and immediately held counsel with the Herodians against him, how to destroy him.

A Great Crowd Follows Jesus

[7]Jesus withdrew with his disciples to the sea, and a great crowd followed, from Galilee and Judea [8]and Jerusalem and Idumea and from beyond the Jordan and from around Tyre and Sidon. When the great crowd heard all that he was doing, they came to him. [9]And he told his disciples to have a boat ready for him because of the crowd, lest they crush him, [10]for he had healed many, so that all who had diseases pressed around him to touch him.

[1]Greek him [a]For 3:1-6 see parallels Matt. 12:9-14; Luke 6:6-11

3:2 The scribes believe that healing is a form of work and thus is not permitted on a **Sabbath. Accuse** is a technical term which means they are looking for legal evidence against Jesus.

3:3-5 To **do good** on the Sabbath would not violate the OT law, but it *would* violate the opponents' Pharisaic tradition. Their tradition misses the point of the Mosaic law: to love God and one's neighbor (see 12:29-31). **Stretch out your hand.** Jesus simply spoke a word, but he did not do anything in this situation that could be called "work."

3:6 The **Pharisees** were quite different from the **Herodians**, who were friends and supporters of the Herodian family dynasty. However, these two groups **held counsel** together (see Ps. 2:2) in order to **destroy** Jesus, who was their common enemy (Mark 14:1-2).

3:7-8 Idumea. The region south of Judea. **beyond the Jordan.** The region east of the Jordan River. **Tyre and Sidon.** The region north of Galilee. All of these regions had belonged to Israel during the time of the judges, and descendants of the 12 tribes had resettled in the area following the Babylonian exile.

[11] And whenever the unclean spirits saw him, they fell down before him and cried out, "You are the Son of God." [12] And he strictly ordered them not to make him known.

The Twelve Apostles

[13] And he went up on the mountain and called to him those whom he desired, and they came to him. [14] And he appointed twelve (whom he also named apostles) so that they might be with him and he might send them out to preach [15] and have authority to cast out demons. [16] He appointed the twelve: [a] Simon (to whom he gave the name Peter); [17] James the son of Zebedee and John the brother of James (to whom he gave the name Boanerges, that is, Sons of Thunder); [18] Andrew, and Philip, and Bartholomew, and Matthew, and Thomas, and James the son of Alphaeus, and Thaddaeus, and Simon the Zealot,[1] [19] and Judas Iscariot, who betrayed him.

[20] Then he went home, and the crowd gathered again, so that they could not even eat. [21] And when his family heard it, they went out to seize him, for they were saying, "He is out of his mind."

[1] Greek *kananaios*, meaning *zealot* [a] For 3:16-19 see parallels Matt. 10:2-4; Luke 6:13-16

3:11–12 Jesus forbids **unclean spirits** to speak about him, so that they will not reveal his true identity before he wants to **make** himself **known**.

3:13–6:6 Jesus' Later Galilean Ministry. Jesus appoints his disciples to teach what he teaches and to do what he does. Parables, nature miracles, and healings expand the range of his authority, which is met with rejection in Nazareth.

3:14–15 Jesus appointed the **twelve**, whom he called out of the larger crowd that had been following him (vv. 7–9). The Twelve have a specific task: (1) that **they might be with him**, and (2) that **he might send them out** (1:17; 9:37). This is why they were called **apostles** (which means "sent out"). They were to (1) **preach** about the kingdom of God (Mark 1:14, 39; 6:12), (2) **cast out demons** (1:34, 39), and (3) heal the sick (6:13). The fact that

Jesus chose 12 apostles is probably related to the 12 tribes of Israel (Rev. 21:14).

3:16–17 The core group of three disciples (see 5:37; 9:2; 14:33) is mentioned first: (**Simon**) Peter, James, and **John**.

3:19 Judas Iscariot, who betrayed him is mentioned last.

3:20 Jesus returns **home**, that is, to the place where he stayed in Capernaum (see note on 2:1).

3:21 The members of Jesus' earthly **family** believe **he is out of his mind** (see John 7:5) because of all that has happened. (Some of Jesus' brothers did later believe in him, notably James, who became the leader of the Jerusalem church, and Judas, probably the same person who wrote the Letter of Jude.)

Blasphemy Against the Holy Spirit

[22] And the scribes who came down from Jerusalem were saying, "He is possessed by Beelzebul," and "by the prince of demons he casts out the demons." [23] [a]And he called them to him and said to them in parables, "How can Satan cast out Satan? [24] If a kingdom is divided against itself, that kingdom cannot stand. [25] And if a house is divided against itself, that house will not be able to stand. [26] And if Satan has risen up against himself and is divided, he cannot stand, but is coming to an end. [27] But no one can enter a strong man's house and plunder his goods, unless he first binds the strong man. Then indeed he may plunder his house.

[28] [b]"Truly, I say to you, all sins will be forgiven the children of man, and whatever blasphemies they utter, [29] but whoever blasphemes against the Holy Spirit never has forgiveness, but is guilty of an eternal sin"— [30] for they were saying, "He has an unclean spirit."

Jesus' Mother and Brothers

[31] [c]And his mother and his brothers came, and standing outside they sent to him and called him. [32] And a crowd was sitting around him, and they said to him, "Your mother and your brothers[1] are outside, seeking you." [33] And he answered them, "Who are my mother and my brothers?" [34] And looking about at those who sat around him, he said, "Here are my mother and my brothers! [35] For whoever does the will of God, he is my brother and sister and mother."

[1] Other manuscripts add and your sisters [a] For 3:23-27 see parallels Matt. 12:25-29; Luke 11:17-22 [b] For 3:28-30 see parallel Matt. 12:31, 32 [c] For 3:31-35 see parallels Matt. 12:46-50; Luke 8:19-21

3:22 Beelzebul. Means "master of the house" and refers to Satan. **by the prince of demons he casts out the demons.** The scribes couldn't deny the reality of the miraculous works Jesus had done, so they attributed his powers to Satan.

3:29 blasphemes against the Holy Spirit. Looking forward to the substitutionary atonement of Jesus, v. 28 emphasized that "all sins will be forgiven." However, if a person persistently gives credit to Satan for what is actually done by the power of God—that is, if a person is convinced that the Holy Spirit's testimony about Jesus is satanic—then such a person never has forgiveness.

3:35 Those who follow Jesus are the true family of

The Parable of the Sower

4 Again [a] he began to teach beside the sea. And a very large crowd gathered about him, so that he got into a boat and sat in it on the sea, and the whole crowd was beside the sea on the land. [2] And he was teaching them many things in parables, and in his teaching he said to them: [3] "Listen! Behold, a sower went out to sow. [4] And as he sowed, some seed fell along the path, and the birds came and devoured it. [5] Other seed fell on rocky ground, where it did not have much soil, and immediately it sprang up, since it had no depth of soil. [6] And when the sun rose, it was scorched, and since it had no root, it withered away. [7] Other seed fell among thorns, and the thorns grew up and choked it, and it yielded no grain. [8] And other seeds fell into good soil and produced grain, growing up and increasing and yielding thirtyfold and sixtyfold and a hundredfold." [9] And he said, "He who has ears to hear, let him hear."

The Purpose of the Parables

[10] And when he was alone, those around him with the twelve asked him about the parables. [11] And he said to them, "To you has been given the secret of the kingdom of God, but for those outside everything is in parables, [12] so that

a For 4:1-12 see parallels Matt. 13:1-15; Luke 8:4-10

God: **whoever does the will of God** (see John 7:17; Rom. 12:2), **he is my brother and sister and mother** (see Heb. 2:11-12).

4:1-34 Mark provides several examples of Jesus teaching in parables. To the hard-hearted, parables are a warning; to those who are open-hearted, they illustrate principles of the messianic rule of God. A parable consists of a story and its corresponding intended message.

4:3-7 a sower went out to sow. Farmers in Bible times sowed their seed without first plowing the ground. Thus the seed fell on various kinds of ground.

4:8 thirtyfold and sixtyfold and a hundredfold. A tenfold return would have been considered a good crop. However, see Gen. 26:12.

4:9 Having **ears to hear** involves giving up one's pride and submitting to God. See Isa. 43:8.

4:11 The secret of the kingdom of God means the nature of God's rule over individuals and over the community of his people. Those who do not (yet) participate in the messianic community are **outside**.

4:12 By quoting Isa. 6:9-10, Jesus is warning that

" 'they may indeed see but not perceive,

and may indeed hear but not understand,

lest they should turn and be forgiven.' "

[13] [a]And he said to them, "Do you not understand this parable? How then will you understand all the parables? [14] The sower sows the word. [15] And these are the ones along the path, where the word is sown: when they hear, Satan immediately comes and takes away the word that is sown in them. [16] And these are the ones sown on rocky ground: the ones who, when they hear the word, immediately receive it with joy. [17] And they have no root in themselves, but endure for a while; then, when tribulation or persecution arises on account of the word, immediately they fall away.[1] [18] And others are the ones sown among thorns. They are those who hear the word, [19] but the cares of the world and the deceitfulness of riches and the desires for other things enter in and choke the word, and it proves unfruitful. [20] But those that were sown on the good soil are the ones who hear the word and accept it and bear fruit, thirtyfold and sixtyfold and a hundredfold."

A Lamp Under a Basket

[21] [b]And he said to them, "Is a lamp brought in to be put under a basket, or under a bed, and not on a stand? [22] For nothing is hidden except to be made manifest; nor is anything secret except to come to light. [23] If anyone has ears to hear, let him hear." [24] And he said to them, "Pay attention to what

[1] Or *stumble* a For 4:13-20 see parallels Matt. 13:18-23; Luke 8:11-15 b For 4:21-25 see parallel Luke 8:16-18

some of those who hear his parables will **hear but not understand**, just like the ancient Israelites.

4:13 How then will you understand? Jesus hints that even the disciples may suffer from hard hearts (see 8:17–18).

4:21-22 The proclamation of the kingdom of God is like bringing an oil **lamp** into a room (see Matt. 5:15). It reveals **hidden** things such as hard hearts.

4:23 ears to hear. See note on v. 9.

4:24-25 If a hearer accepts Jesus' message of the

you hear: with the measure you use, it will be measured to you, and still more will be added to you. [25] For to the one who has, more will be given, and from the one who has not, even what he has will be taken away."

The Parable of the Seed Growing

[26] And he said, "The kingdom of God is as if a man should scatter seed on the ground. [27] He sleeps and rises night and day, and the seed sprouts and grows; he knows not how. [28] The earth produces by itself, first the blade, then the ear, then the full grain in the ear. [29] But when the grain is ripe, at once he puts in the sickle, because the harvest has come."

The Parable of the Mustard Seed

[30] [a] And he said, "With what can we compare the kingdom of God, or what parable shall we use for it? [31] It is like a grain of mustard seed, which, when sown on the ground, is the smallest of all the seeds on earth, [32] yet when it is sown it grows up and becomes larger than all the garden plants and puts out large branches, so that the birds of the air can make nests in its shade."

[33] With many such parables he spoke the word to them, as they were able to hear it. [34] He did not speak to them without a parable, but privately to his own disciples he explained everything.

[a] For 4:30-32 see parallels Matt. 13:31, 32; Luke 13:18, 19

kingdom, then God will give an increased **measure** of understanding and blessing.

4:26–29 The people of Jesus' day expected God's kingdom to come suddenly, but Jesus tells them it will begin in a small way (**first the blade, then the ear**) and then will grow slowly but steadily amid adversity. It will reach its full growth and glory only at the second coming of Jesus. See note on vv. 30–32.

4:29 Sickle and harvest are symbolic language for the last judgment (see Joel 3:13).

4:30–32 A third **parable** teaches that the **kingdom** of God begins in a small and unnoticed way, which is not what the people expected (see note on vv. 26–29). A **mustard seed**, the smallest of all agricultural seeds in Palestine, could produce a bush as large as 3 by 12 feet (0.9 by 3.7 m). The nesting of **birds** in the shadow of the grown bush is a picture of divine blessing (see Ps. 91:1–2).

4:34 He did not speak to them without a parable means that Jesus regularly included parables in his teaching. It does not mean he spoke only in parables.

Jesus Calms a Storm

35 [a] On that day, when evening had come, he said to them, "Let us go across to the other side." **36** And leaving the crowd, they took him with them in the boat, just as he was. And other boats were with him. **37** And a great windstorm arose, and the waves were breaking into the boat, so that the boat was already filling. **38** But he was in the stern, asleep on the cushion. And they woke him and said to him, "Teacher, do you not care that we are perishing?" **39** And he awoke and rebuked the wind and said to the sea, "Peace! Be still!" And the wind ceased, and there was a great calm. **40** He said to them, "Why are you so afraid? Have you still no faith?" **41** And they were filled with great fear and said to one another, "Who then is this, that even the wind and the sea obey him?"

Jesus Heals a Man with a Demon

5 [b] They came to the other side of the sea, to the country of the Gerasenes.[1] **2** And when Jesus[2] had stepped out of the boat, immediately there met him out of the tombs a man with an unclean spirit. **3** He lived among the tombs. And no one could bind him anymore, not even with a chain, **4** for he had often been bound with shackles and chains, but he wrenched the chains apart, and he broke the shackles in pieces. No one had the strength to subdue him. **5** Night and day among the tombs and on the mountains he was always

---

[1] Some manuscripts *Gergesenes*; some *Gadarenes* [2] Greek *he*; also verse 9 [a] For 4:35-41 see parallels Matt. 8:18, 23-27; Luke 8:22-25 [b] For 5:1-20 see parallels Matt. 8:28-34; Luke 8:26-39

. . . .

4:36 A **boat** dated from the first century AD was found in the Sea of Galilee in 1986. Approximately 26.5 feet long and 7.5 feet wide (8 m by 2.3 m), it could hold about 15 people.

4:37 The Sea of Galilee is 696 feet (212 m) below sea level, resulting in sudden storms (**windstorm**; see 6:48).

4:38 Asleep on the cushion is an eyewitness detail included only in Mark's account of this incident. He was probably told about it by Peter (see Introduction: Author, Date, and Recipients). Jesus' sleeping indicates lack of fear and also great fatigue—a reminder that he was fully human as well as fully divine.

4:39 Peace! Be still! Jesus displays his divine power over nature (cf. Ps. 107:25-30; Amos 4:13).

4:40 afraid. The cure for fear is **faith** in Jesus.

crying out and cutting himself with stones. [6] And when he saw Jesus from afar, he ran and fell down before him. [7] And crying out with a loud voice, he said, "What have you to do with me, Jesus, Son of the Most High God? I adjure you by God, do not torment me." [8] For he was saying to him, "Come out of the man, you unclean spirit!" [9] And Jesus asked him, "What is your name?" He replied, "My name is Legion, for we are many." [10] And he begged him earnestly not to send them out of the country. [11] Now a great herd of pigs was feeding there on the hillside, [12] and they begged him, saying, "Send us to the pigs; let us enter them." [13] So he gave them permission. And the unclean spirits came out and entered the pigs; and the herd, numbering about two thousand, rushed down the steep bank into the sea and drowned in the sea.

[14] The herdsmen fled and told it in the city and in the country. And people came to see what it was that had happened. [15] And they came to Jesus and saw the demon-possessed[1] man, the one who had had the legion, sitting there, clothed and in his right mind, and they were afraid. [16] And those who had seen it described to them what had happened to the demon-possessed man and to the pigs. [17] And they began to beg Jesus[2] to depart from their region. [18] As he was getting into the boat, the man who had been possessed

[1] Greek *daimonizomai* (demonized); also verses 16, 18; elsewhere rendered *oppressed by demons* [2] Greek *him*

5:6–7 Ran and fell down before Jesus may mean that the demons unwillingly submitted to Jesus' greater power, or that the man himself longed to be free of the demonic influence, or some of both.

5:8 Was saying (imperfect tense) indicates that Jesus had told the demon more than once to **come out of the man**, but it had not obeyed.

5:9 My name is Legion. A legion was the largest unit of the Roman army, with as many as 6,000 soldiers. This does not necessarily mean that there were 6,000 demons in the man, only that there were a great **many**.

5:11 It is not surprising to find ceremonially unclean **pigs** in the Gentile Decapolis region.

5:13 The herd of **pigs** (about 2,000) would have been raised for food in this Gentile region on the east shore of the Sea of Galilee.

5:15 they were afraid. The townspeople seem to have had a superstitious fear of Jesus' mysterious power. Perhaps they were also afraid of losing more property.

5:18–20 that he might be with him. It is possible that the restored man was asking Jesus for permission to join the inner circle of disciples (see 3:14), but Jesus wanted him to be a witness to God's power **in the Decapolis.** Jesus often discouraged such publicity, so that the people would not try to make him a political messiah. But apparently Jesus knew that the Gentile

with demons begged him that he might be with him. [19] And he did not permit him but said to him, "Go home to your friends and tell them how much the Lord has done for you, and how he has had mercy on you." [20] And he went away and began to proclaim in the Decapolis how much Jesus had done for him, and everyone marveled.

Jesus Heals a Woman and Jairus's Daughter

[21] And when Jesus had crossed again in the boat to the other side, a great crowd gathered about him, and he was beside the sea. [22][a] Then came one of the rulers of the synagogue, Jairus by name, and seeing him, he fell at his feet [23] and implored him earnestly, saying, "My little daughter is at the point of death. Come and lay your hands on her, so that she may be made well and live." [24] And he went with him.

And a great crowd followed him and thronged about him. [25] And there was a woman who had had a discharge of blood for twelve years, [26] and who had suffered much under many physicians, and had spent all that she had, and was no better but rather grew worse. [27] She had heard the reports about Jesus and came up behind him in the crowd and touched his garment. [28] For she said, "If I touch even his garments, I will be made well." [29] And immediately the flow of blood dried up, and she felt in her body that she was healed of her disease. [30] And Jesus, perceiving in himself that power

a For 5:22-43 see parallels Matt. 9:18-26; Luke 8:40-56

people of the Decapolis would not do this. The work of the **Lord** in Mark 5:19 is described as the work of **Jesus** in v. 20, indicating that Jesus shares the same nature as God himself.

5:21 to the other side. Jesus returns to the Galilean side of the sea.

5:22 The laymen who were **rulers of the synagogue** presided over the affairs of the synagogue, including organizing and teaching in synagogue services.

Most of them were Pharisees (on synagogues The Synagogue and Jewish Worship, pp. 156–157).

5:25–27 discharge of blood. On account of her condition, the woman is ceremonially unclean (see Lev. 15:25–28). She is not permitted to enter the temple section reserved for women, or to be in public without making people aware of her condition. **touched his garment.** Jesus makes the woman clean by his power, instead of becoming unclean himself (see Lev. 15:19–23; Mark 1:41; 5:41).

had gone out from him, immediately turned about in the crowd and said, "Who touched my garments?" **31** And his disciples said to him, "You see the crowd pressing around you, and yet you say, 'Who touched me?'" **32** And he looked around to see who had done it. **33** But the woman, knowing what had happened to her, came in fear and trembling and fell down before him and told him the whole truth. **34** And he said to her, "Daughter, your faith has made you well; go in peace, and be healed of your disease."

35 While he was still speaking, there came from the ruler's house some who said, "Your daughter is dead. Why trouble the Teacher any further?" **36** But overhearing[1] what they said, Jesus said to the ruler of the synagogue, "Do not fear, only believe." **37** And he allowed no one to follow him except Peter and James and John the brother of James. **38** They came to the house of the ruler of the synagogue, and Jesus[2] saw a commotion, people weeping and wailing loudly. **39** And when he had entered, he said to them, "Why are you making a commotion and weeping? The child is not dead but sleeping." **40** And they laughed at him. But he put them all outside and took the child's father and mother and those who were with him and went in where the child was. **41** Taking her by the hand he said to her, "Talitha cumi," which means, "Little girl, I say to you, arise." **42** And

[1] Or *ignoring*; some manuscripts *hearing* [2] Greek *he*

5:31-33 Fear and trembling can lead to faith.

5:34 The Greek word for **made (you) well** can mean either "heal" or "save."

5:35 Verses 35-43 resume the account of Jairus's daughter (vv. 22-24).

5:36 Do not fear, only believe. Again, Jesus shows that faith is the solution to fear (see 2:5; 4:40).

5:37 Peter and James and John. Only the inner circle of disciples is permitted to join Jesus (see 1:29; 9:2; and note on 3:16-17).

5:38-40 weeping and wailing loudly. Some in the crowd were professional mourners, who were expected to be present even at funerals for the poor. **The child is not dead but sleeping.** The child had indeed died (see Luke 8:55), but from Jesus' viewpoint her death is but sleep.

5:41 Touching a dead person renders one ceremonially unclean (Lev. 22:4; Num. 19:11), but once again Jesus overcomes uncleanness (see note on Mark 5:25-27), and the girl comes back to life (see 2 Kings 4:17-37; Acts 9:39-41). **Talitha cumi.** At times, Mark reports Jesus' statements in Aramaic, which shows that Mark's writing was based on eyewitness accounts.

immediately the girl got up and began walking (for she was twelve years of age), and they were immediately overcome with amazement. [43] And he strictly charged them that no one should know this, and told them to give her something to eat.

Jesus Rejected at Nazareth

6 [a] He went away from there and came to his hometown, and his disciples followed him. [2] And on the Sabbath he began to teach in the synagogue, and many who heard him were astonished, saying, "Where did this man get these things? What is the wisdom given to him? How are such mighty works done by his hands? [3] Is not this the carpenter, the son of Mary and brother of James and Joses and Judas and Simon? And are not his sisters here with us?" And they took offense at him. [4] And Jesus said to them, "A prophet is not without honor, except in his hometown and among his relatives and in his own household." [5] And he could do no mighty work there, except that he laid his hands on a few sick people and healed them. [6] And he marveled because of their unbelief.

And he went about among the villages teaching.

[a] For 6:1-6 see parallel Matt. 13:54-58

5:43 no one should know this. See note on Mark 1:44.

6:1-2 synagogue. See The Synagogue and Jewish Worship, pp. 156–157. Jesus was most likely asked to give a message following the reading of Scripture (cf. Luke 4:16–30, which was probably the same incident). **Where did this man get these things?** Until he began his ministry, Jesus' divine nature was hidden. Even people in his hometown, who had known him since childhood, had no idea that he was also fully God.

6:3 Is not this . . . the son of Mary may hint that some people thought Jesus was an illegitimate child. Joseph must have had at least four sons, among whom were **James** (see Acts 12:17; Gal. 1:19; 2:9, 12) and **Judas** (not the betrayer), as well as at least two daughters.

6:4 Like other prophets before him (e.g., 2 Chron. 36:16; Jer. 11:21; Mark 6:17), Jesus is not honored by his own family or by his **hometown**.

6:5-6 could do no mighty work there. Jesus will not force his miracles on a hostile, skeptical audience. Nevertheless, he continues **teaching** (see 1:22; 4:1, 2; 6:2, etc.).

Jesus Sends Out the Twelve Apostles

[7] [a]And he called the twelve and began to send them out two by two, and gave them authority over the unclean spirits. [8] He charged them to take nothing for their journey except a staff—no bread, no bag, no money in their belts— [9] but to wear sandals and not put on two tunics.[1] [10] And he said to them, "Whenever you enter a house, stay there until you depart from there. [11] And if any place will not receive you and they will not listen to you, when you leave, shake off the dust that is on your feet as a testimony against them." [12] So they went out and proclaimed that people should repent. [13] And they cast out many demons and anointed with oil many who were sick and healed them.

The Death of John the Baptist

[14] [b]King Herod heard of it, for Jesus'[2] name had become known. Some[3] said, "John the Baptist[4] has been raised from the dead. That is why these miraculous powers are at work in him." [15] But others said, "He is Elijah."

---

[1] Greek chiton, a long garment worn under the cloak next to the skin [2] Greek his [3] Some manuscripts He [4] Greek baptizer; also verse 24 [a] For 6:7-11 see parallels Matt. 10:1, 5, 9-14; Luke 9:1, 3-5 [b] For 6:14-29 see parallels Matt. 14:1-12; Luke 9:7-9

....

6:7–8:26 Work beyond Galilee. The disciples are sent out to spread the message of God's kingdom, to heal, and to cast out demons. Jesus again demonstrates his authority and warns his disciples against hard hearts.

6:7–13 Jesus sends out **the twelve** disciples to proclaim repentance (vv. 10–12), cast out unclean spirits (v. 7), and heal (v. 13). See 3:14–15.

6:8–9 no bread, no bag, no money in their belts. These provisions are to come from people who repent upon hearing the disciples' message.

6:11 Jews who returned from Gentile regions were to **shake off the dust that is on** their **feet** as a form of cleansing. Here the action also serves as a sign **against** towns that reject God's message.

6:13 Oil was commonly used in prayer for healing.

6:14–56 The death of John the Baptist casts an ominous shadow on Jesus' future. Jesus' life is in danger, partly because of his authoritative, miraculous deeds.

6:14a Herod Antipas served under Rome as an administrator of Galilee and Perea (4 BC–AD 39). He was not technically a **King**, although his contemporaries may have referred to him as such (see v. 23).

6:14b–15 The list of popular beliefs about Jesus includes that he is (1) the revived **John the Baptist**, (2) the expected **Elijah** (see Mal. 3:1–2; 4:5–6), or (3) **one of the prophets.** Many Jews expected that Elijah, who was caught up to heaven without dying (2 Kings 2:11), would return at the end of time. (See Mark 9:11–13; Luke 1:17.) The third belief—that Jesus

And others said, "He is a prophet, like one of the prophets of old." [16] But when Herod heard of it, he said, "John, whom I beheaded, has been raised." [17] For it was Herod who had sent and seized John and bound him in prison for the sake of Herodias, his brother Philip's wife, because he had married her. [18] For John had been saying to Herod, "It is not lawful for you to have your brother's wife." [19] And Herodias had a grudge against him and wanted to put him to death. But she could not, [20] for Herod feared John, knowing that he was a righteous and holy man, and he kept him safe. When he heard him, he was greatly perplexed, and yet he heard him gladly.

[21] But an opportunity came when Herod on his birthday gave a banquet for his nobles and military commanders and the leading men of Galilee. [22] For when Herodias's daughter came in and danced, she pleased Herod and his guests. And the king said to the girl, "Ask me for whatever you wish, and I will give it to you." [23] And he vowed to her, "Whatever you ask me, I will give you, up to half of my kingdom." [24] And she went out and said to her mother, "For what should I ask?" And she said, "The head of John the Baptist." [25] And she came in immediately with haste to the king and asked, saying, "I want you to give me at once the head of John the Baptist on a platter." [26] And the king was exceedingly sorry, but because of his oaths and his guests he did not want to break his word to her. [27] And immediately the king sent an executioner with orders to bring John's[1] head. He went and

[1] Greek his

was "a prophet, like one of the prophets of old"— might have been based on Deut. 18:15, 18.

6:17 John the Baptist had publicly charged **Herod Antipas** with breaking the law by marrying **Herodias**, the former **wife** of his still living half brother (see Lev. 18:16; 20:21). In response, Herod had put John **in prison**.

6:18 **It is not lawful.** Even though Herod Antipas was

not a Jew, John did not hesitate to tell him he had violated God's moral law (see Lev. 18:16).

6:19–20 **Herod feared John.** Perhaps he feared an uprising on account of John's popularity (1:5). Or perhaps he feared divine punishment for his sin.

6:23 **Up to half of my kingdom** should be seen as a figure of speech rather than a literal promise.

beheaded him in the prison [28] and brought his head on a platter and gave it to the girl, and the girl gave it to her mother. [29] When his disciples heard of it, they came and took his body and laid it in a tomb.

Jesus Feeds the Five Thousand

[30] The apostles returned to Jesus and told him all that they had done and taught. [31] And he said to them, "Come away by yourselves to a desolate place and rest a while." For many were coming and going, and they had no leisure even to eat. [32] [a]And they went away in the boat to a desolate place by themselves. [33] Now many saw them going and recognized them, and they ran there on foot from all the towns and got there ahead of them. [34] When he went ashore he saw a great crowd, and he had compassion on them, because they were like sheep without a shepherd. And he began to teach them many things. [35] And when it grew late, his disciples came to him and said, "This is a desolate place, and the hour is now late. [36] Send them away to go into the surrounding countryside and villages and buy themselves something to eat." [37] But he answered them, "You give them something to eat." And they said to him, "Shall we go and buy two hundred denarii[1] worth of bread and give it to them to eat?" [38] And he said to them, "How many loaves do you have? Go and see." And when they had found out, they said, "Five, and two fish." [39] Then he commanded them all to sit down in groups on the green grass. [40] So they sat down in groups, by hundreds and by fifties. [41] And taking the five loaves and the two fish, he looked up

[1] A *denarius* was a day's wage for a laborer   a For 6:32-44 see parallels Matt. 14:13-21; Luke 9:10-17; John 6:1-13

6:30 returned. See vv. 7–13.

6:34 like sheep without a shepherd. See Num. 27:17; Ezek. 34:4–5. Jesus teaches the people, functioning as the good shepherd (cf. Ps. 23:1–4; Isa. 40:11; Jer. 23:4).

6:36–37 Two hundred denarii represented 200 days' wages for a laborer.

6:41–42 As God provided manna in the desert, so Jesus provides food in a deserted place. The feeding of the 5,000 reinforces Jesus' proclamation:

to heaven and said a blessing and broke the loaves and gave them to the disciples to set before the people. And he divided the two fish among them all. [42] And they all ate and were satisfied. [43] And they took up twelve baskets full of broken pieces and of the fish. [44] And those who ate the loaves were five thousand men.

Jesus Walks on the Water

[45][a] Immediately he made his disciples get into the boat and go before him to the other side, to Bethsaida, while he dismissed the crowd. [46] And after he had taken leave of them, he went up on the mountain to pray. [47] And when evening came, the boat was out on the sea, and he was alone on the land. [48] And he saw that they were making headway painfully, for the wind was against them. And about the fourth watch of the night[1] he came to them, walking on the sea. He meant to pass by them, [49] but when they saw him walking on the sea they thought it was a ghost, and cried out, [50] for they all saw him and were terrified. But immediately he spoke to them and said, "Take heart; it is I. Do not be afraid." [51] And he got into the boat with them, and the wind ceased. And they were utterly astounded, [52] for they did not understand about the loaves, but their hearts were hardened.

[1] That is, between 3 A.M. and 6 A.M. [a] For 6:45-52 see parallels Matt. 14:22-33; John 6:16-21

after feeding them the Word of God (v. 34), he miraculously provides physical food.

6:43 they took up twelve baskets full. As with the miracles of Elijah and Elisha (see 1 Kings 17:16; 2 Kings 4:7, 42–44), much food is left over. Jesus did not want any food to be wasted.

6:45 Bethsaida was just northeast of where the Jordan flows into the Sea of Galilee from the north.

6:48 fourth watch. 3:00 a.m. to 6:00 a.m. The Sea of Galilee is 696 feet (212 m) below sea level, resulting in violent downdrafts and sudden windstorms (see 4:37). Jesus sees the disciples' need and walks on water toward them (cf. Job 9:8; Ps. 77:20; Isa. 43:16). **He meant to pass by them,** not to avoid them, but so that they would see him walking on the water. The passage echoes the incident where God "passed" before Moses (Ex. 33:19, 22; 34:6), giving a glimpse of his glory. See Job 9:11, where Job says that God "passes by" him. By walking on the water, Jesus is essentially proclaiming his deity.

6:49–50 "It is I" echoes Ex. 3:14.

6:51–52 Even though Jesus had multiplied the **loaves** and had walked on the water, the disciples' **hearts were hardened** and they didn't realize who he was. See 8:18–21.

Jesus Heals the Sick in Gennesaret

53 [a] When they had crossed over, they came to land at Gennesaret and moored to the shore. **54** And when they got out of the boat, the people immediately recognized him **55** and ran about the whole region and began to bring the sick people on their beds to wherever they heard he was. **56** And wherever he came, in villages, cities, or countryside, they laid the sick in the marketplaces and implored him that they might touch even the fringe of his garment. And as many as touched it were made well.

Traditions and Commandments

7 [b] Now when the Pharisees gathered to him, with some of the scribes who had come from Jerusalem, **2** they saw that some of his disciples ate with hands that were defiled, that is, unwashed. **3** (For the Pharisees and all the Jews do not eat unless they wash their hands properly,[1] holding to the tradition of the elders, **4** and when they come from the marketplace, they do not eat unless they wash.[2] And there are many other traditions that they observe, such as the washing of cups and pots and copper vessels and dining couches.[3]) **5** And the Pharisees and the scribes asked him, "Why do your disciples not walk according to the tradition of the elders, but eat with defiled hands?" **6** And he said to them, "Well did Isaiah prophesy of you hypocrites, as it is written,

[1] Greek unless they wash the hands with a fist, probably indicating a kind of ceremonial washing [2] Greek unless they baptize; some manuscripts unless they purify themselves [3] Some manuscripts omit and dining couches [a] For 6:53-56 see parallel Matt. 14:34-36 [b] For 7:1-30 see parallel Matt. 15:1-28

....

6:53 The northeasterly wind had caused the ship to drift southwestward, bringing them to **Gennesaret** instead of their intended destination of Bethsaida.

7:1-23 Conflict arises between the Pharisees and Jesus over the issue of true moral purity.

7:5 Scribes are sent from Jerusalem (v. 1) to investigate the situation brought about by Jesus' popularity. **eat with defiled hands.** The disciples are not breaking the Mosaic law but rather the **tradition of the elders** that prescribed ritual washing of hands, utensils, and furniture (see vv. 2-4). By his example, Jesus implies that his disciples may ignore these traditions (see Luke 11:37-38).

[a]" 'This people honors me with their lips,

>> but their heart is far from me;

7 >> in vain do they worship me,

>> teaching as doctrines the commandments of men.'

[8] You leave the commandment of God and hold to the tradition of men."

[9] And he said to them, "You have a fine way of rejecting the commandment of God in order to establish your tradition! [10] For Moses said, [b] 'Honor your father and your mother'; and, [c] 'Whoever reviles father or mother must surely die.' [11] But you say, 'If a man tells his father or his mother, "Whatever you would have gained from me is Corban"' (that is, given to God)[1]— [12] then you no longer permit him to do anything for his father or mother, [13] thus making void the word of God by your tradition that you have handed down. And many such things you do."

What Defiles a Person

[14] And he called the people to him again and said to them, "Hear me, all of you, and understand: [15] There is nothing outside a person that by going into him can defile him, but the things that come out of a person are what defile him."[2] [17] And when he had entered the house and left the people, his disciples asked him about the parable. [18] And he said to them, "Then are you also without understanding? Do you not see that whatever

[1] Or an offering [2] Some manuscripts add verse 16: If anyone has ears to hear, let him hear [a] Isa. 29:13 [b] Ex. 20:12 [c] Ex. 21:17

7:10–13 honor your father and your mother (see Ex. 20:12; 21:17; Deut. 5:16). Jewish tradition allowed that funds committed for the care of parents could be declared **Corban** ("dedicated to God"; see Lev. 1:2; 2:1). This would mean that the person no longer had to give anything to his parents. **thus making void the word of God**. The Corban tradition was just one example of a "tradition of men" that nullified an important "commandment of God" (Mark 7:8; see Ex. 20:12).

7:15 can defile him. The problem of the defiled human heart is much more serious than mere ceremonial impurity (see Jer. 17:9–10). Throughout Scripture, the heart refers to the center of one's being, including the mind, emotions, and will (see Prov. 4:23).

goes into a person from outside cannot defile him, [19] since it enters not his heart but his stomach, and is expelled?"[1] (Thus he declared all foods clean.) [20] And he said, "What comes out of a person is what defiles him. [21] For from within, out of the heart of man, come evil thoughts, sexual immorality, theft, murder, adultery, [22] coveting, wickedness, deceit, sensuality, envy, slander, pride, foolishness. [23] All these evil things come from within, and they defile a person."

The Syrophoenician Woman's Faith

[24] And from there he arose and went away to the region of Tyre and Sidon.[2] And he entered a house and did not want anyone to know, yet he could not be hidden. [25] But immediately a woman whose little daughter had an unclean spirit heard of him and came and fell down at his feet. [26] Now the woman was a Gentile, a Syrophoenician by birth. And she begged him to cast the demon out of her daughter. [27] And he said to her, "Let the children be fed first, for it is not right to take the children's bread and throw it to the dogs." [28] But she answered him, "Yes, Lord; yet even the dogs under the table eat the children's crumbs." [29] And he said to her, "For this statement

---

[1] Greek goes out into the latrine [2] Some manuscripts omit and Sidon

....

7:19 declared all foods clean. The Mosaic ceremonial laws distinguished between "clean" and "unclean" foods (see Lev. 11:1–47). The purpose of these laws was to make people aware of their sin as a barrier to fellowship with a holy God. But after Jesus, through his atoning death, made possible the forgiveness of sins and full fellowship with God, the ceremonial laws would no longer be required.

7:24–30 Jesus went first to the people of Israel. However, these verses foreshadow the future ministry of the disciples to the Gentiles.

7:24 did not want anyone to know. See note on Mark 1:44. Jesus was already known in the Gentile region of **Tyre and Sidon**, where there were many resettled Jews (see note on Mark 3:7–8). Jesus was called first to proclaim God's kingdom to the

people of Israel, but he also spoke of a time when his disciples would take the gospel to the Gentiles (13:10; 14:9).

7:26 Elijah had also helped a non-Jewish woman in this area (1 Kings 17:8). **Syrophoenician.** A native of Phoenicia, which included Tyre and Sidon.

7:27 Jesus' response is surprising and may seem offensive. Taking into account vv. 29–30, one can conclude that Jesus spoke as he did merely to test the woman's faith.

7:28–30 yet even the dogs. The woman's response to Jesus' surprising statement (v. 27) is both humble and persistent. Perhaps she understands and humbly accepts that God called Israel first for a particular purpose (see Ex. 4:22).

you may go your way; the demon has left your daughter." [30] And she went home and found the child lying in bed and the demon gone.

Jesus Heals a Deaf Man

[31] Then he returned from the region of Tyre and went through Sidon to the Sea of Galilee, in the region of the Decapolis. [32] And they brought to him a man who was deaf and had a speech impediment, and they begged him to lay his hand on him. [33] And taking him aside from the crowd privately, he put his fingers into his ears, and after spitting touched his tongue. [34] And looking up to heaven, he sighed and said to him, "Ephphatha," that is, "Be opened." [35] And his ears were opened, his tongue was released, and he spoke plainly. [36] And Jesus[1] charged them to tell no one. But the more he charged them, the more zealously they proclaimed it. [37] And they were astonished beyond measure, saying, "He has done all things well. He even makes the deaf hear and the mute speak."

Jesus Feeds the Four Thousand

8 [a] In those days, when again a great crowd had gathered, and they had nothing to eat, he called his disciples to him and said to them, [2] "I have compassion on the crowd, because they have been with me now three days and have nothing to eat. [3] And if I send them away hungry to their homes, they will faint on the way. And some of them have come from far away." [4] And his disciples answered him, "How can one feed these people with bread here in

[1] Greek he a For 8:1-10 see parallel Matt. 15:32-39

7:31-8:26 As Jesus continues his ministry of teaching and healing, the disciples' hearts remain hard (8:17-21). They fail to understand who Jesus really is.

7:33 Unlike his other healings, Jesus uses physical means to heal the man. This allows him to illustrate the problem of spiritual deafness and blindness (see 8:17-18, 21).

7:36 to tell no one. See 1:45; 5:20, 34; 8:26; and note on 1:44.

8:1-10 The feeding of the 4,000 probably took

this desolate place?" [5] And he asked them, "How many loaves do you have?" They said, "Seven." [6] And he directed the crowd to sit down on the ground. And he took the seven loaves, and having given thanks, he broke them and gave them to his disciples to set before the people; and they set them before the crowd. [7] And they had a few small fish. And having blessed them, he said that these also should be set before them. [8] And they ate and were satisfied. And they took up the broken pieces left over, seven baskets full. [9] And there were about four thousand people. And he sent them away. [10] And immediately he got into the boat with his disciples and went to the district of Dalmanutha.[1]

The Pharisees Demand a Sign

[11] [a] The Pharisees came and began to argue with him, seeking from him a sign from heaven to test him. [12] And he sighed deeply in his spirit and said, "Why does this generation seek a sign? Truly, I say to you, no sign will be given to this generation." [13] And he left them, got into the boat again, and went to the other side.

The Leaven of the Pharisees and Herod

[14] Now they had forgotten to bring bread, and they had only one loaf with them in the boat. [15] And he cautioned them, saying, "Watch out; beware

---

[1] Some manuscripts *Magadan*, or *Magdala*   [a] For 8:11-21 see parallel Matt. 16:1-12

place in Gentile territory. Jesus is the living bread for Gentiles as well as for Jews.

8:5 The number **seven** is usually symbolic of perfection or completion. Here the number may symbolize the fullness of God's provision for all peoples, including Gentiles.

8:6 Giving **thanks**, breaking bread, and distributing it are common elements in a Jewish meal.

8:8 **satisfied. . . . left over, seven baskets full.** Jesus provides beyond satisfaction (cf. 6:43).

8:11 The Pharisees demand not just a miracle but a **sign from heaven.** But they didn't have the one thing that Jesus required: a fundamental change of heart.

8:12 **sighed.** For other examples of Jesus expressing emotions, see 1:41; 3:5; 7:34. **this generation.** Cf. Deut. 32:5; Ps. 95:10; Mark 9:19. **no sign.** For the person who has an open heart, Jesus' miracles should be more than enough to show that he truly is the Messiah.

8:13 In v. 10, Jesus crossed the Sea of Galilee traveling west; now he crosses it again, traveling east.

8:14–15 Jesus uses **leaven** to describe the self-centered, self-reliant **Pharisees** and **Herod** Antipas.

of the leaven of the Pharisees and the leaven of Herod."[1] [16] And they began discussing with one another the fact that they had no bread. [17] And Jesus, aware of this, said to them, "Why are you discussing the fact that you have no bread? Do you not yet perceive or understand? Are your hearts hardened? [18] Having eyes do you not see, and having ears do you not hear? And do you not remember? [19] When I broke the five loaves for the five thousand, how many baskets full of broken pieces did you take up?" They said to him, "Twelve." [20] "And the seven for the four thousand, how many baskets full of broken pieces did you take up?" And they said to him, "Seven." [21] And he said to them, "Do you not yet understand?"

Jesus Heals a Blind Man at Bethsaida

[22] And they came to Bethsaida. And some people brought to him a blind man and begged him to touch him. [23] And he took the blind man by the hand and led him out of the village, and when he had spit on his eyes and laid his hands on him, he asked him, "Do you see anything?" [24] And he looked up and said, "I see people, but they look like trees, walking." [25] Then Jesus[2] laid his hands on his eyes again; and he opened his eyes, his sight was restored, and he saw everything clearly. [26] And he sent him to his home, saying, "Do not even enter the village."

[1] Some manuscripts *the Herodians* [2] Greek *he*

Leaven is fermented dough. Leftover dough was often added to a new lump of dough.

8:16 had no bread. The disciples take the term "leaven" (v. 15) literally, showing their ongoing inability to understand spiritual truths (see vv. 17–21).

8:17–18 not yet perceive or understand. While the Pharisees reject Jesus' teaching outright, the disciples are slow to appreciate it. The figurative reference to **eyes** and **ears** echoes the healings of the deaf (7:31–35) and blind (8:22–26) men. Jesus wants to open the "ears" and "eyes" of the disciples' hearts.

8:21 Now that Jesus has twice multiplied food, the disciples should **understand** the significance of these miracles: he who stands before them is none other than the eternal creator and giver of life (see Col. 1:15–20).

8:23–25 Jesus led the blind man **out of the village**, perhaps to get away from hostile onlookers (see 5:40; 6:6). The blind man's first response, "**I see people, but they look like trees, walking**," could be seen as similar to the disciples' lack of understanding (8:17–21).

Peter Confesses Jesus as the Christ

²⁷ ᵃAnd Jesus went on with his disciples to the villages of Caesarea Philippi. And on the way he asked his disciples, "Who do people say that I am?" ²⁸ And they told him, "John the Baptist; and others say, Elijah; and others, one of the prophets." ²⁹ And he asked them, "But who do you say that I am?" Peter answered him, "You are the Christ." ³⁰ And he strictly charged them to tell no one about him.

Jesus Foretells His Death and Resurrection

³¹ ᵇAnd he began to teach them that the Son of Man must suffer many things and be rejected by the elders and the chief priests and the scribes and be killed, and after three days rise again. ³² And he said this plainly. And Peter took him aside and began to rebuke him. ³³ But turning and seeing his disciples, he rebuked Peter and said, "Get behind me, Satan! For you are not setting your mind on the things of God, but on the things of man."

ᵃ For 8:27-29 see parallels Matt. 16:13-16; Luke 9:18-20 ᵇ For 8:31–9:1 see parallels Matt. 16:21-28; Luke 9:22-27

8:27–16:8 Testing Jesus' Authority in Suffering. Having displayed his messianic authority and power (1:1–8:26), Jesus is now tested as the Messiah of God.

8:27–10:52 Journey to Jerusalem. As Jesus and his disciples journey toward Jerusalem, he warns them three times about his approaching death and teaches them about the cost of discipleship.

8:27–29a Caesarea Philippi is some 25 miles (40 km) north of the Sea of Galilee. It had been a center of the worship of (1) Baal, then (2) the Greek god Pan, and then (3) Caesar. At this time it was an important Greco-Roman city. It had a primarily pagan Syrian and Greek population. **Who do people say that I am?** Jesus' questions prepare the disciples for his teaching. He must show them that the Messiah of God is to be humbled (Mark 8:31; 10:45) and then exalted (8:38) for the sake of his people. This goes against popular messianic expectations. On **John the Baptist** and **Elijah**, see note on 6:14b–15.

8:29b–30 Peter speaks for the Twelve (cf. 1:36; 8:32; 9:5; 10:28; 14:29) and confesses Jesus as **the Christ**, the Messiah (2 Sam. 7:14–16; Psalm 2; Jer. 23:5–6) who they expect will liberate the Jewish people from Rome. Peter's confession is God-given (Matt. 16:17) but incomplete, for Jesus will also suffer for his people (Isa. 53:1–12; Mark 8:31; 10:45). This is why Jesus charges his disciples to **tell no one about him.**

8:31 must . . . be killed. Christ's death is necessary because the messianic rule of God must begin with atonement for sin. Christ's death will be the sacrifice that brings reconciliation between God and man. That Jesus would **rise again** must puzzle the disciples. They expect only the general resurrection of all mankind at the end of the age, prior to judgment (Dan. 12:2).

8:33 turning and seeing his disciples, he rebuked Peter. The fact that Jesus looked at all the disciples implies that his rebuke of Peter was intended for all of them. **"Get behind me, Satan!"** It is only Peter's thoughts and words (see v. 32), not him personally, that Jesus rejects as satanic.

³⁴ And calling the crowd to him with his disciples, he said to them, "If anyone would come after me, let him deny himself and take up his cross and follow me. ³⁵ For whoever would save his life[1] will lose it, but whoever loses his life for my sake and the gospel's will save it. ³⁶ For what does it profit a man to gain the whole world and forfeit his soul? ³⁷ For what can a man give in return for his soul? ³⁸ For whoever is ashamed of me and of my words in this adulterous and sinful generation, of him will the Son of Man also be ashamed when he comes in the glory of his Father with the holy angels."

9 And he said to them, "Truly, I say to you, there are some standing here who will not taste death until they see the kingdom of God after it has come with power."

The Transfiguration

²ᵃAnd after six days Jesus took with him Peter and James and John, and led them up a high mountain by themselves. And he was transfigured before them, ³ and his clothes became radiant, intensely white, as no one[2] on earth could bleach them. ⁴ And there appeared to them Elijah with Moses, and

[1] The same Greek word can mean either *soul* or *life*, depending on the context; twice in this verse and once in verse 36 and once in verse 37 [2] Greek *launderer (gnapheus)* [a] For 9:2-8 see parallels Matt. 17:1-8; Luke 9:28-36

8:34 Following the first major prediction of his death and resurrection (v. 31), Jesus gives instructions in discipleship to all those who **would come after me**. They should deny themselves and take up their **cross** so that they will be free to **follow** the Messiah (1:18). Each of the major predictions of Jesus' death and resurrection is followed by teaching on discipleship (8:33–9:1; 9:33–50; 10:38–45).

8:35 Jesus' teaching here involves a paradox: The person who lives a self-centered life (**would save his life**) will not find eternal life with God (**will lose it**), but the person who gives up his self-centered life (**loses his life**) for the **sake** of Christ and the gospel will find everlasting life with God (**will save it**; see v. 38).

8:38 of him will the Son of Man also be ashamed. Jesus claims divine authority in final judgment.

9:1 Some standing here who will not taste death probably refers to the three disciples who will accompany Jesus to the Mount of Transfiguration. They will see **the kingdom of God . . . come with power**. The transfiguration is a "preview" of the glory of Christ in his return (Dan. 7:13–27; Mark 13:26–27).

9:2 high mountain. Church tradition identifies this as Mount Tabor, about 12 miles (19 km) from the Sea of Galilee. Most scholars favor Mount Hermon, outside of Galilee and rising 9,166 feet (2,794 m) above sea level.

9:3 On white as heavenly brightness, compare Dan. 7:9; Luke 24:4; Acts 1:10; Rev. 1:14.

9:4 Jesus is greater than both **Moses**, who represents the Law, and **Elijah**, who represents the Prophets. Jesus thus fulfills both the Law and the Prophets (see Matt. 5:17). Luke adds the detail that they discuss Jesus' imminent "departure" (Luke 9:31).

they were talking with Jesus. [5] And Peter said to Jesus, "Rabbi,[1] it is good

that we are here. Let us make three tents, one for you and one for Moses and

one for Elijah." [6] For he did not know what to say, for they were terrified.

[7] And a cloud overshadowed them, and a voice came out of the cloud, "This

is my beloved Son;[2] listen to him." [8] And suddenly, looking around, they no

longer saw anyone with them but Jesus only.

[9] [a] And as they were coming down the mountain, he charged them to

tell no one what they had seen, until the Son of Man had risen from the

dead. [10] So they kept the matter to themselves, questioning what this rising

from the dead might mean. [11] And they asked him, "Why do the scribes

say that first Elijah must come?" [12] And he said to them, "Elijah does come

first to restore all things. And how is it written of the Son of Man that he

should suffer many things and be treated with contempt? [13] But I tell you

that Elijah has come, and they did to him whatever they pleased, as it is

written of him."

[1] *Rabbi* means *my teacher*, or *my master* [2] Or *my Son, my* (or *the*) *Beloved* [a] For 9:9-13 see parallel Matt. 17:9-13

9:5 Peter sees Jesus merely as someone similar to **Moses** and **Elijah** and wishes to raise **tents** for them, perhaps because he wants to prolong the experience. Peter does not know what he is saying, for he is speaking impulsively, out of fear (v. 6).

9:7 The **voice . . . out of the cloud** echoes Ex. 24:15–16. **This is my beloved Son; listen to him.** Jesus, with all his claims, is endorsed by the Father (see Ps. 2:7; Isa. 42:1; Mark 1:11). "Listen to him" echoes Deut. 18:15, 18, where Moses is shown to be a leader-prophet.

9:9 tell no one. See note on Mark 1:44. Jesus commands silence in order to avoid a popular movement that would make him into a political "freedom fighter" (see John 6:15). Such a political role would interfere with his purpose of suffering and dying to save his people.

9:10 questioning what this rising from the dead might mean. The disciples expected only the resurrection of all mankind at the end of this age, after the coming of Elijah (see Dan. 12:2).

9:12 John the Baptist restored **all things** by preparing the way for the coming of the ultimate Restorer (see Mal. 3:1; Luke 1:17; Acts 3:21). Malachi reveals that the future messenger will have a prophetic ministry like Elijah's. The NT identifies John the Baptist as the fulfillment of Malachi's prophesied Elijah. **be treated with contempt.** See Isa. 53:3.

9:13 Referring to John the Baptist, Jesus states that **Elijah has come.** See Luke 1:17. Jesus thus contradicted popular expectations (Mark 9:11), which hoped for the literal return of Elijah.

Jesus Heals a Boy with an Unclean Spirit

[14][a]And when they came to the disciples, they saw a great crowd around them, and scribes arguing with them. [15]And immediately all the crowd, when they saw him, were greatly amazed and ran up to him and greeted him. [16]And he asked them, "What are you arguing about with them?" [17]And someone from the crowd answered him, "Teacher, I brought my son to you, for he has a spirit that makes him mute. [18]And whenever it seizes him, it throws him down, and he foams and grinds his teeth and becomes rigid. So I asked your disciples to cast it out, and they were not able." [19]And he answered them, "O faithless generation, how long am I to be with you? How long am I to bear with you? Bring him to me." [20]And they brought the boy to him. And when the spirit saw him, immediately it convulsed the boy, and he fell on the ground and rolled about, foaming at the mouth. [21]And Jesus asked his father, "How long has this been happening to him?" And he said, "From childhood. [22]And it has often cast him into fire and into water, to destroy him. But if you can do anything, have compassion on us and help us." [23]And Jesus said to him, "'If you can'! All things are possible for one who believes." [24]Immediately the father of the child cried out[1] and said, "I believe; help my unbelief!" [25]And when Jesus saw that a crowd came running together, he rebuked the unclean spirit, saying to it, "You mute and deaf spirit, I command you, come out of him and never enter him again." [26]And after crying out and convulsing him terribly, it came out, and the boy was like a corpse, so that most of them said, "He is dead." [27]But Jesus

[1] Some manuscripts add *with tears*   [a] For 9:14-28 see parallels Matt. 17:14-19; Luke 9:37-42

9:19 O faithless generation. Jesus' burdened expression echoes that of the prophets (e.g., Deut. 32:5, 20; Isa. 6:11; Jer. 5:21–22; see note on Mark 8:12).

9:22b–24 The father is merely seeking a miracle from Jesus (**if you can do anything**), but Jesus calls on him to put his trust in God.

took him by the hand and lifted him up, and he arose. [28] And when he had entered the house, his disciples asked him privately, "Why could we not cast it out?" [29] And he said to them, "This kind cannot be driven out by anything but prayer."[1]

Jesus Again Foretells Death, Resurrection

[30] [a] They went on from there and passed through Galilee. And he did not want anyone to know, [31] for he was teaching his disciples, saying to them, "The Son of Man is going to be delivered into the hands of men, and they will kill him. And when he is killed, after three days he will rise." [32] But they did not understand the saying, and were afraid to ask him.

Who Is the Greatest?

[33] And they came to Capernaum. And when he was in the house [b] he asked them, "What were you discussing on the way?" [34] But they kept silent, for on the way they had argued with one another about who was the greatest. [35] And he sat down and called the twelve. And he said to them, "If anyone would be first, he must be last of all and servant of all." [36] And he took a child and put him in the midst of them, and taking him in his arms, he said

[1] Some manuscripts add *and fasting* [a] For 9:30-32 see parallels Matt. 17:22, 23; Luke 9:43-45 [b] For 9:33-37 see parallels Matt. 18:1-5; Luke 9:46-48

. . . .

9:28-29 "Why could we not cast it out?" The disciples lack the ability to fully carry out their commission from Jesus (see 6:7, 13; 9:18).

9:30-31 he did not want anyone to know. Jesus seeks privacy in order to continue **teaching his disciples** about his impending suffering in Jerusalem (see note on Mark 1:44).

9:32 The disciples do not **understand** that Jesus, the Messiah, must die; rather, they expect the Messiah to be a political liberator. Nor do they understand the idea of individual resurrection; they expect only the resurrection of all mankind at the last judgment (see Dan. 12:2). Yet they understand enough of what Jesus is saying that they are **afraid to ask him** anything more. Perhaps they remember that, when

Peter expressed disapproval of Jesus' predictions of suffering, Jesus rebuked him (Mark 8:33).

9:33 in the house. Jesus instructs the disciples in the privacy of the home (see 4:10, 34; 7:17; 9:28; 10:10).

9:34 who was the greatest. Because they thought the Messiah would be a political liberator, the disciples dream of status, honor, and power.

9:35 he sat down. Teachers often sat as they taught.

9:36-37 Jesus shows the disciples that, instead of seeking greater status (v. 34), they should be willing to take on lowly, often unnoticed tasks. They should care for those who have little status in the world, such as a little **child. receives not me.**

to them, [37] "Whoever receives one such child in my name receives me, and whoever receives me, receives not me but him who sent me."

Anyone Not Against Us Is for Us

[38] [a] John said to him, "Teacher, we saw someone casting out demons in your name,[1] and we tried to stop him, because he was not following us." [39] But Jesus said, "Do not stop him, for no one who does a mighty work in my name will be able soon afterward to speak evil of me. [40] For the one who is not against us is for us. [41] For truly, I say to you, whoever gives you a cup of water to drink because you belong to Christ will by no means lose his reward.

Temptations to Sin

[42] "Whoever causes one of these little ones who believe in me to sin,[2] it would be better for him if a great millstone were hung around his neck and he were thrown into the sea. [43] And if your hand causes you to sin, cut it off. It is better for you to enter life crippled than with two hands to go to hell,[3] to the unquenchable fire.[4] [45] And if your foot causes you to sin, cut it off. It is better for you to enter life lame than with two feet to be thrown into hell. [47] And if your eye causes you to sin, tear it out. It is better for you to enter the kingdom of God with one eye than with two eyes to be thrown into hell, [48] 'where their worm does not die and the fire is not quenched.'

---

[1] Some manuscripts add who does not follow us   [2] Greek to stumble; also verses 43, 45, 47   [3] Greek Gehenna; also verse 47   [4] Some manuscripts add verses 44 and 46 (which are identical with verse 48)   [a] For 9:38-40 see parallel Luke 9:49, 50

An example of "step parallelism," in which the first thought is raised a step higher in the second thought: a child is received as a representative of Jesus; Jesus is received as a representative of God.

9:40 the one who is not against us is for us. Cf. Phil. 1:17–18. For a contrasting but equally true statement, see Matt. 12:30.

9:41 will by no means lose his reward. God notices the smallest of deeds.

9:42 Any who cause other believers, especially the lowly or powerless, **to sin** will receive severe punishment from God.

9:43–48 Jesus uses hyperbole (intentional overstatement) to show the seriousness of **sin**: nothing, even important things such as a **hand, foot,** or **eye,** can be more important than God. Of course, Jesus does not mean that people should literally cut off those body parts, for the literal removal of them cannot remove the root of sin in the heart (see 7:20–23; 9:45).

⁴⁹ For everyone will be salted with fire.[1] ⁵⁰ Salt is good, but if the salt has lost its saltiness, how will you make it salty again? Have salt in yourselves, and be at peace with one another."

Teaching About Divorce

10 ᵃAnd he left there and went to the region of Judea and beyond the Jordan, and crowds gathered to him again. And again, as was his custom, he taught them.

² And Pharisees came up and in order to test him asked, "Is it lawful for a man to divorce his wife?" ³ He answered them, "What did Moses command you?" ⁴ They said, "Moses allowed a man to write a certificate of divorce and to send her away." ⁵ And Jesus said to them, "Because of your hardness of heart he wrote you this commandment. ⁶ But from the beginning of creation, 'God made them ᵇ male and female.' ⁷ ᶜ'Therefore a man shall leave his father and mother and hold fast to his wife,[2] ⁸ and the two shall become one flesh.' So they are no longer two but one flesh. ⁹ What therefore God has joined together, let not man separate."

¹⁰ And in the house the disciples asked him again about this matter. ¹¹ And he said to them, "Whoever divorces his wife and marries another

[1] Some manuscripts add *and every sacrifice will be salted with salt* [2] Some manuscripts omit *and hold fast to his wife*
ᵃ For 10:1-12 see parallel Matt. 19:1-9 ᵇ Gen. 1:27; 5:2 ᶜ Gen. 2:24

9:49 Everyone will be salted with fire is a puzzling statement that occurs only in Mark. In view of Lev. 2:13, "with all your offerings you shall offer salt," perhaps the best interpretation is that believers are being offered to God (cf. Rom. 12:1), and the fire with which they will be "salted" is purification by the "fire" of suffering and hardship.

9:50 lost its saltiness. Most salt came from the Dead Sea and contained impurities. If not processed properly, it would have a poor taste and be unusable for food. If the conditions of discipleship are not kept, the disciples likewise will become worthless.

10:1 And he left there. Jesus sets out on his final journey from Galilee to Jerusalem. He returns to the area north of Jericho where his ministry began. He continues to focus his ministry on teaching, **as was his custom.**

10:2 Jesus' Pharisaic opponents hope to expose him as an opponent of the Law of Moses.

10:4-6 Jesus emphasizes that marriage goes back to God's purpose at the **beginning of creation** (Gen. 1:27; 2:24; Ex. 20:14). Moses' regulations on divorce (Deut. 24:1-4) were not part of God's original plan but were instituted **because of your hardness of heart.**

10:10-11 in the house. Once again, Jesus instructs

commits adultery against her, [12] and if she divorces her husband and marries another, she commits adultery."

Let the Children Come to Me

[13] [a]And they were bringing children to him that he might touch them, and the disciples rebuked them. [14] But when Jesus saw it, he was indignant and said to them, "Let the children come to me; do not hinder them, for to such belongs the kingdom of God. [15] Truly, I say to you, whoever does not receive the kingdom of God like a child shall not enter it." [16] And he took them in his arms and blessed them, laying his hands on them.

The Rich Young Man

[17] [b]And as he was setting out on his journey, a man ran up and knelt before him and asked him, "Good Teacher, what must I do to inherit eternal life?" [18] And Jesus said to him, "Why do you call me good? No one is good except God alone. [19] You know the commandments: [c]'Do not murder, Do not commit adultery, Do not steal, Do not bear false witness, Do not defraud, Honor your father and mother.'" [20] And he said to him, "Teacher, all these

[a] For 10:13-16 see parallels Matt. 19:13-15; Luke 18:15-17 [b] For 10:17-31 see parallels Matt. 19:16-30; Luke 18:18-30
[c] Ex. 20:12-16; Deut. 5:16-20

his disciples in private (see 4:10; 9:33). **Whoever divorces his wife and marries another.** Here and in Luke 16:18 Jesus does not include the phrase "except for sexual immorality" as in Matt. 5:32 and 19:9. The most likely reason is that everyone agreed that **adultery** was a legitimate ground for divorce, and Jesus is not addressing that issue here.

10:12 And if she divorces her husband is the only time in the Gospels where it is assumed that a woman also has a right to initiate a divorce (compare 1 Cor. 7:10–11), as Roman culture allowed.

10:13–15 rebuked them. The disciples consider **children** to be an annoying distraction (see 9:36–37, 42). To Jesus, however, **children** are as important as adults, and equally worthy of love (9:36–37; 10:16). **to such belongs the kingdom of God.** Children do

not belong automatically to the kingdom but must **come to Jesus** and **receive** him the same as adults.

10:17–27 Contrary to childlike trust (vv. 13–16), the rich young **man** relies on his **possessions** (v. 22) and his self-righteousness (v. 20) to **inherit eternal life.**

10:18 No one is completely **good except God alone,** therefore it is not proper for the young man to address Jesus as "Good Teacher" until he is ready to acknowledge that Jesus is God.

10:19 Do not defraud probably combines the eighth and ninth commandments ("not steal. . . . not bear false witness," Ex. 20:15–16).

10:20 all these I have kept. From a human perspective, the young man's answer is plausible (cf. Paul, prior to his conversion; Phil. 3:6). However, once the righteousness of God sheds light on the human

I have kept from my youth." [21] And Jesus, looking at him, loved him, and said to him, "You lack one thing: go, sell all that you have and give to the poor, and you will have treasure in heaven; and come, follow me." [22] Disheartened by the saying, he went away sorrowful, for he had great possessions.

[23] And Jesus looked around and said to his disciples, "How difficult it will be for those who have wealth to enter the kingdom of God!" [24] And the disciples were amazed at his words. But Jesus said to them again, "Children, how difficult it is[1] to enter the kingdom of God! [25] It is easier for a camel to go through the eye of a needle than for a rich person to enter the kingdom of God." [26] And they were exceedingly astonished, and said to him,[2] "Then who can be saved?" [27] Jesus looked at them and said, "With man it is impossible, but not with God. For all things are possible with God." [28] Peter began to say to him, "See, we have left everything and followed you." [29] Jesus said, "Truly, I say to you, there is no one who has left house or brothers or sisters or mother or father or children or lands, for my sake and for the gospel, [30] who will not receive a hundredfold now in this time, houses and brothers and sisters and mothers and children and lands, with persecutions, and in the age to come eternal life. [31] But many who are first will be last, and the last first."

[1] Some manuscripts add *for those who trust in riches* [2] Some manuscripts *to one another*

condition (see Rom. 3:21–26; Phil. 3:7–11), human righteousness is seen to be no more than a thin cover-up for mankind's basic hostility toward God (Col. 1:21).

10:21 You lack one thing. The man has replaced trust in God and its reward (**treasure in heaven**) with trust in earthly riches. He thus fails the first commandment, "You shall have no other gods before me" (Ex. 20:3). This does not mean that every disciple of Christ must **sell all** that he has; rather, the heart must be focused on God, with every possession available for his use.

10:22 he went away sorrowful. The man's true state has been laid bare, but he does not repent.

10:25 The hyperbole (intentional overstatement) of a large **camel** having to fit through the small **eye of a needle** stresses that such a thing is humanly impossible (but see v. 27). For other hyperboles in Jesus' teaching, see Matt. 7:3–5; 23:24.

10:29–30 The person who leaves **house, lands,** and family **for Jesus' sake** (see 8:35, 38; Matt. 5:11; Luke 12:8–9; 18:29) **and for the gospel** can expect **now** in this life to enjoy fellowship with other believers. He will find a welcome in the **houses** and **lands** of Christian friends. But in this life these blessings will be mixed with **persecutions** (see Mark 8:34–38). The future will yield an even better reward: **eternal life.**

Jesus Foretells His Death a Third Time

32 [a] And they were on the road, going up to Jerusalem, and Jesus was walking ahead of them. And they were amazed, and those who followed were afraid. And taking the twelve again, he began to tell them what was to happen to him, **33** saying, "See, we are going up to Jerusalem, and the Son of Man will be delivered over to the chief priests and the scribes, and they will condemn him to death and deliver him over to the Gentiles. **34** And they will mock him and spit on him, and flog him and kill him. And after three days he will rise."

The Request of James and John

35 [b] And James and John, the sons of Zebedee, came up to him and said to him, "Teacher, we want you to do for us whatever we ask of you." **36** And he said to them, "What do you want me to do for you?" **37** And they said to him, "Grant us to sit, one at your right hand and one at your left, in your glory." **38** Jesus said to them, "You do not know what you are asking. Are you able to drink the cup that I drink, or to be baptized with the baptism with which I am baptized?" **39** And they said to him, "We are able." And Jesus said to them, "The cup that I drink you will drink, and with the baptism with which I

a For 10:32-34 see parallels Matt. 20:17-19; Luke 18:31-33   b For 10:35-45 see parallel Matt. 20:20-28

10:32–45 Each of Jesus' major predictions of his death and resurrection (8:31; 9:30-31; 10:33-34) is followed by instruction in discipleship (8:33–9:1; 9:33-50; 10:38-45).

10:32 Jesus is aware that he will soon be put to death (see 8:31; 9:31; Isa. 53:1-12), but he proceeds resolutely toward Jerusalem. He is like the servant of the Lord in Isa. 50:7, who set his face "like a flint" (cf. Luke 9:53, "his face was set").

10:35–37 James and John belonged to Jesus' "inner circle" (see 1:29; 5:37). They falsely envisioned special places of honor (one at your right hand and one at your left) when Jesus would rule in Jerusalem on the throne of David.

10:38 The cup that Jesus was to drink was the cup of God's wrath that would be poured out on him, as he bore God's wrath in the place of sinful mankind. His baptism was his suffering and death, which would pour over him like a flood.

10:39 The disciples understand Jesus' question ("Are you able to drink the cup that I drink?" v. 38) to mean that they will need to fight alongside Jesus. They bravely answer, We are able. Jesus, however, teaches them that they too will undergo suffering: you will drink . . . you will be baptized.

am baptized, you will be baptized, [40] but to sit at my right hand or at my left is not mine to grant, but it is for those for whom it has been prepared." [41] And when the ten heard it, they began to be indignant at James and John. [42] And Jesus called them to him and said to them, "You know that those who are considered rulers of the Gentiles lord it over them, and their great ones exercise authority over them. [43] But it shall not be so among you. But whoever would be great among you must be your servant,[1] [44] and whoever would be first among you must be slave[2] of all. [45] For even the Son of Man came not to be served but to serve, and to give his life as a ransom for many."

Jesus Heals Blind Bartimaeus

[46] [a]And they came to Jericho. And as he was leaving Jericho with his disciples and a great crowd, Bartimaeus, a blind beggar, the son of Timaeus, was sitting by the roadside. [47] And when he heard that it was Jesus of Nazareth, he began to cry out and say, "Jesus, Son of David, have mercy on me!" [48] And many rebuked him, telling him to be silent. But he cried out all the more, "Son of David, have mercy on me!" [49] And Jesus stopped and said, "Call him." And they called the blind man, saying to him, "Take heart. Get up;

[1] Greek *diakonos* [2] Or *bondservant,* or *servant* (for the contextual rendering of the Greek word *doulos,* see Preface)
[a] For 10:46-52 see parallels Matt. 20:29-34; Luke 18:35-43

10:40 *is not mine to grant.* Though Jesus is fully God, there are differences of authority within the Trinity. Throughout Scripture, the Son is always subject to the authority of the Father, who will ultimately determine who receives such positions of honor.

10:41 The other disciples become **indignant at James and John,** perhaps on account of their own ambition and jealousy (vv. 42–45).

10:42 *lord it over.* Jesus does not deny all human authority (cf. Matt. 16:19; 18:18), only its oppressive misuse.

10:45 The *ransom* of Christ's life was paid to God the Father, who accepted it as just payment for the sins of **many** (all who would be saved). See Isa. 53:8–12; Rom. 4:25; 1 Cor. 15:3; 1 Tim. 2:5–6. **Son of Man.** See note on Mark 2:27–28.

For an additional resource on the Passion predictions in Mark, see p. 155.

10:46–52 Both 8:22–26 and this passage tell of the healing of a blind man. The disciples were themselves blind regarding the true mission of Jesus, but between these two accounts of healing, Jesus has taught them and has discussed his death and resurrection. As he taught them, he was healing their spiritual blindness as well.

10:46 *Jericho.* Not the ancient OT city (Joshua 5–6), but the new Jericho, about a mile (1.6 km) to the south of the older city.

10:47 Jesus will later say that the cry of the blind man (**Jesus, Son of David, have mercy on me**) was

he is calling you." **50** And throwing off his cloak, he sprang up and came to

Jesus. **51** And Jesus said to him, "What do you want me to do for you?" And

the blind man said to him, "Rabbi, let me recover my sight." **52** And Jesus

said to him, "Go your way; your faith has made you well." And immediately

he recovered his sight and followed him on the way.

The Triumphal Entry

11 *a*Now when they drew near to Jerusalem, to Bethphage and Bethany, at

the Mount of Olives, Jesus¹ sent two of his disciples **2** and said to them, "Go

into the village in front of you, and immediately as you enter it you will find

a colt tied, on which no one has ever sat. Untie it and bring it. **3** If anyone says

to you, 'Why are you doing this?' say, 'The Lord has need of it and will send it

back here immediately.' " **4** And they went away and found a colt tied at a door

outside in the street, and they untied it. **5** And some of those standing there

said to them, "What are you doing, untying the colt?" **6** And they told them

what Jesus had said, and they let them go. **7** And they brought the colt to Jesus

and threw their cloaks on it, and he sat on it. **8** And many spread their cloaks

on the road, and others spread leafy branches that they had cut from the

fields. **9** And those who went before and those who followed were shouting,

¹ Greek *he* ᵃ For 11:1-10 see parallels Matt. 21:1-9; Luke 19:28-38; John 12:12-15

an expression of faith (v. 52). "Son of David" is a messianic acclamation (see 12:35–37).

10:52 Your faith has made you well hints at spiritual salvation as well; see note on 5:34. **and followed him.** Bartimaeus joins Jesus and the other pilgrims on their final journey to Jerusalem; he has become one of Jesus' disciples.

11:1–13:37 Entering and Judging Jerusalem. Jesus enters Jerusalem triumphantly, cleanses the temple, and authoritatively teaches both opponents and disciples.

11:2 Matthew mentions that a donkey was with the colt (see Matt. 21:6–7).

11:7 By riding on a donkey, Jesus fulfills a prophecy about the Messiah (Zech. 9:9).

11:8 Cloaks on the road symbolized the crowd's submission to Jesus as king (see 2 Kings 9:13). **Branches** (palms) symbolized Jewish nationalism and victory (see John 12:13).

11:9 Hosanna. "Save!" **Blessed is he who comes in the name of the Lord** is from Ps. 118:25–26, a prayer of blessing for the coming messianic kingdom. The Triumphal Entry takes place at the beginning of Passover week, which recalls the Jewish people's liberation from Egyptian slavery (see note on Mark 14:17). The pilgrims now are anticipating liberation from Rome's oppression. But rather than defeating

"Hosanna! Blessed is he who comes in the name of the Lord! [10] Blessed is the coming kingdom of our father David! Hosanna in the highest!"

[11] And he entered Jerusalem and went into the temple. And when he had looked around at everything, as it was already late, he went out to Bethany with the twelve.

Jesus Curses the Fig Tree

[12] On the following day, when they came from Bethany, he was hungry. [13] And seeing in the distance a fig tree in leaf, he went to see if he could find anything on it. When he came to it, he found nothing but leaves, for it was not the season for figs. [14] And he said to it, "May no one ever eat fruit from you again." And his disciples heard it.

Jesus Cleanses the Temple

[15] [a] And they came to Jerusalem. And he entered the temple and began to drive out those who sold and those who bought in the temple, and he overturned the tables of the money-changers and the seats of those who sold pigeons. [16] And he would not allow anyone to carry anything through the temple. [17] And he was teaching them and saying to them, "Is it not written, [b] 'My

[a] For 11:15-18 see parallels Matt. 21:12-16; Luke 19:45-47   [b] Isa. 56:7

Rome, Jesus will defeat Satan, sin, and death. This celebration fulfills Zech. 9:9.

11:11 As the sovereign Lord who "will suddenly come to his temple" (Mal. 3:1), Jesus **looked around at everything** in the temple area. During this week, Jesus and the Twelve stay a short distance outside Jerusalem in **Bethany**, probably with their friends Lazarus, Mary, and Martha (see John 12:2–3).

11:12–12:44 Jesus' first actions, after being hailed by the people as King, are to pass judgment on Jerusalem figuratively through the cursing of the fig tree and to cleanse the temple. These actions show his zeal for true worship of God.

11:13–14 Since the fruit of the fig tree begins to appear about the same time as the leaves, the appearance of leaves in full bloom means that the figs should already have been growing. But Jesus **found nothing but leaves** on the fig tree. This symbolizes the hypocrisy of those who seem to be bearing fruit but in fact are not. Jesus has in mind especially Israel, since in the OT the **fig tree** often serves as a symbol for Israel (e.g., Jer. 8:13; Hos. 9:10, 16; Joel 1:7).

11:15–17 he entered the temple. Jesus comes as Lord of the temple, to purify it (Mal. 3:1–4). **Tables** had been set up in the temple area to enable pilgrims to change their various currencies into coins for the annual temple tax, as well as to purchase **pigeons**, lambs, oil, salt, etc., for various sacrifices. But the business activity had turned the temple into a **den of robbers** (Jer. 7:11). Gentiles in particular were hindered by the commerce in the outer temple court. Jesus wants to restore the temple to its function as **a house of prayer for all the nations** (Isa. 56:7).

house shall be called a house of prayer for all the nations'? But you have made it a den of robbers." [18] And the chief priests and the scribes heard it and were seeking a way to destroy him, for they feared him, because all the crowd was astonished at his teaching. [19] And when evening came they[1] went out of the city.

The Lesson from the Withered Fig Tree

[20] [a]As they passed by in the morning, they saw the fig tree withered away to its roots. [21] And Peter remembered and said to him, "Rabbi, look! The fig tree that you cursed has withered." [22] And Jesus answered them, "Have faith in God. [23] Truly, I say to you, whoever says to this mountain, 'Be taken up and thrown into the sea,' and does not doubt in his heart, but believes that what he says will come to pass, it will be done for him. [24] Therefore I tell you, whatever you ask in prayer, believe that you have received[2] it, and it will be yours. [25] And whenever you stand praying, forgive, if you have anything against anyone, so that your Father also who is in heaven may forgive you your trespasses."[3]

The Authority of Jesus Challenged

[27] [b]And they came again to Jerusalem. And as he was walking in the temple, the chief priests and the scribes and the elders came to him, [28] and

[1] Some manuscripts he [2] Some manuscripts are receiving [3] Some manuscripts add verse 26: But if you do not forgive, neither will your Father who is in heaven forgive your trespasses [a] For 11:20-24 see parallel Matt. 21:19-22 [b] For 11:27-33 see parallels Matt. 21:23-27; Luke 20:1-8

11:18 they feared him. The Jewish leaders correctly saw Jesus' act as a challenge to their authority in the most sacred space in the world.

11:20 Mark reports that the disciples did not see the withered fig tree until the next **morning**. Matthew compresses the events of these two days into a single story (Matt. 21:18–22).

11:21 The withered **fig tree** represents God's judgment on Israel (see note on vv. 13–14).

11:22-23 Moving a **mountain** was symbolic language for doing the seemingly impossible (cf. Isa. 40:4; 54:10).

11:24-25 believe that you have received it, and it will

be yours. Some have misunderstood this to mean that if they pray for some specific request and have enough faith, then God will do whatever they ask. But while we must always trust in God's power, we must also submit to his will (14:36). Those who trust God for the right things in the right way can have confidence that God will "supply every need . . . according to his riches in glory in Christ Jesus" (Phil. 4:19; see also Rom. 8:28, 32).

11:28-33 by what authority. The question relates to the cleansing of the temple (vv. 15–19) but also to Jesus' healing and teaching throughout his ministry, since he is neither a recognized priest nor an official interpreter of the law. **Was the baptism of**

they said to him, "By what authority are you doing these things, or who gave you this authority to do them?" [29] Jesus said to them, "I will ask you one question; answer me, and I will tell you by what authority I do these things. [30] Was the baptism of John from heaven or from man? Answer me." [31] And they discussed it with one another, saying, "If we say, 'From heaven,' he will say, 'Why then did you not believe him?' [32] But shall we say, 'From man'?"—they were afraid of the people, for they all held that John really was a prophet. [33] So they answered Jesus, "We do not know." And Jesus said to them, "Neither will I tell you by what authority I do these things."

The Parable of the Tenants

12 [a]And he began to speak to them in parables. "A man planted a vineyard and put a fence around it and dug a pit for the winepress and built a tower, and leased it to tenants and went into another country. [2] When the season came, he sent a servant[1] to the tenants to get from them some of the fruit of the vineyard. [3] And they took him and beat him and sent him away empty-handed. [4] Again he sent to them another servant, and they struck him on the head and treated him shamefully. [5] And he sent another, and him they killed. And so with many others: some they beat, and some they killed. [6] He had still one other, a beloved son. Finally he sent him to them, saying,

[1] Or bondservant; also verse 4 [a] For 12:1-12 see parallels Matt. 21:33-46; Luke 20:9-18

John from heaven or from man? This confession of ignorance by Jesus' opponents demonstrates that they have no basis on which to judge his ministry.

12:1-12 This parable of judgment is addressed primarily to the religious leaders of Israel (vv. 1, 12). Disputes between absentee landlords, their representatives (a servant), and tenants were common in Israel (vv. 3-5). The vineyard is a well-known symbol for Israel (Neh. 9:16-37; Isa. 5:1-5).

12:1 vineyard, fence, tower. The landlord goes to great expense, so he is justified in expecting a share in the profit.

12:3-5 The landlord's servants are increasingly mistreated: they are beaten, struck . . . on the head, and killed. The repetition of these events (and so with many others) reinforces the injustice. While Israel might have borne fruit, the leaders of Israel have prevented the fruit from being given to God.

12:6 The tenants' attitude toward the landlord will be directly reflected in their respect, or lack of it, for his beloved son, who represents Jesus (1:11; 9:7).

'They will respect my son.' ⁷ But those tenants said to one another, 'This is

the heir. Come, let us kill him, and the inheritance will be ours.' ⁸ And they

took him and killed him and threw him out of the vineyard. ⁹ What will the

owner of the vineyard do? He will come and destroy the tenants and give

the vineyard to others. ¹⁰ Have you not read this Scripture:

> ᵃ" 'The stone that the builders rejected
>
>   has become the cornerstone;¹
>
> ¹¹   this was the Lord's doing,
>
>   and it is marvelous in our eyes'?"

¹² And they were seeking to arrest him but feared the people, for they

perceived that he had told the parable against them. So they left him and

went away.

Paying Taxes to Caesar

¹³ ᵇAnd they sent to him some of the Pharisees and some of the Herodians,

to trap him in his talk. ¹⁴ And they came and said to him, "Teacher, we know

that you are true and do not care about anyone's opinion. For you are not

swayed by appearances,² but truly teach the way of God. Is it lawful to pay

---

¹ Greek *the head of the corner* ² Greek *you do not look at people's faces* ª Ps. 118:22, 23 ᵇ For 12:13-27 see parallels Matt. 22:15-32; Luke 20:20-38

12:7 kill. They may be assuming that the heir's arrival means the landlord has died.

12:9 give the vineyard to others. Israel (and the Son sent to her) belongs to God. Israel's leaders disrespect the possessions of God (11:27-12:12) and thus incur the judgment of God.

12:10 In Jesus' day, Ps. 118:22-23 was seen as messianic (see Acts 4:11). Jesus' opponents can thus understand that the "stone" refers to the Messiah. **Builders** refers to the leaders of Israel. **Rejected** echoes the theme of the persecution of

the prophets of God (Neh. 9:9-35; Acts 7:1-53). The new Israel (faithful Israel) will accept the Son as the rightful messenger, heir, and **cornerstone** of the messianic kingdom (Jer. 51:16; Zech. 4:7).

12:13 The **Pharisees** and **Herodians** collaborate against Jesus (see note on 3:6). Although the Herodians and the Pharisees were on different sides of many political and religious issues, they join forces here to combat what they see as a threat to their power and status.

12:14 Is it lawful to pay taxes? Refusing to pay taxes

taxes to Caesar, or not? Should we pay them, or should we not?" [15] But, knowing their hypocrisy, he said to them, "Why put me to the test? Bring me a denarius[1] and let me look at it." [16] And they brought one. And he said to them, "Whose likeness and inscription is this?" They said to him, "Caesar's." [17] Jesus said to them, "Render to Caesar the things that are Caesar's, and to God the things that are God's." And they marveled at him.

The Sadducees Ask About the Resurrection

[18] And Sadducees came to him, who say that there is no resurrection. And they asked him a question, saying, [19] "Teacher, Moses wrote for us that if a man's brother dies and leaves a wife, but leaves no child, the man[2] must take the widow and raise up offspring for his brother. [20] There were seven brothers; the first took a wife, and when he died left no offspring. [21] And the second took her, and died, leaving no offspring. And the third likewise. [22] And the seven left no offspring. Last of all the woman also died. [23] In the resurrection, when they rise again, whose wife will she be? For the seven had her as wife."

[24] Jesus said to them, "Is this not the reason you are wrong, because you know neither the Scriptures nor the power of God? [25] For when they rise from the dead, they neither marry nor are given in marriage, but are like

---

[1] A *denarius* was a day's wage for a laborer   [2] Greek *his brother*

to Rome would seem to entail rebellion against Caesar. But a willingness to pay taxes would seem to compromise devotion to God.

12:16 The likeness and inscription on the denarius represent the person of Caesar and his authority. Simply by having the coin, Jesus' opponents show that they already participate in the Roman social order.

12:17 the things that are Caesar's . . . the things that are God's. Jesus does not discuss the question of whether the current Roman government is just or unjust, but he does imply that it is right

to pay taxes to **Caesar**. God's kingdom, however, transcends all of these "things."

12:18–23 The Sadducees, who reject any belief in the resurrection of the dead, try to show how such a belief would be in conflict with the law about levirate marriage (Deut. 25:5–6). How, they ask, can one woman be married to seven men in heaven?

12:25 The Sadducees falsely assume there will be marriage in **heaven**. Interpersonal relationships in heaven are similar to the relationships of angels (whose existence the Sadducees deny; see Acts 23:8). This teaching might at first seem

angels in heaven. [26] And as for the dead being raised, have you not read in the book of Moses, in the passage about the bush, how God spoke to him, saying, [a]'I am the God of Abraham, and the God of Isaac, and the God of Jacob'? [27] He is not God of the dead, but of the living. You are quite wrong."

The Great Commandment

[28] [b]And one of the scribes came up and heard them disputing with one another, and seeing that he answered them well, asked him, "Which commandment is the most important of all?" [29] Jesus answered, "The most important is, [c]'Hear, O Israel: The Lord our God, the Lord is one. [30] And you shall love the Lord your God with all your heart and with all your soul and with all your mind and with all your strength.' [31] The second is this: [d]'You shall love your neighbor as yourself.' There is no other commandment greater than these." [32] And the scribe said to him, "You are right, Teacher. You have truly said that he is one, and there is no other besides him. [33] And to love him with all the heart and with all the understanding and with all the strength, and to love one's neighbor as oneself, is much more than all whole burnt offerings and sacrifices." [34] And when Jesus saw that he answered wisely, he said to him, "You are not far from the kingdom of God." And after that no one dared to ask him any more questions.

[a] Ex. 3:6 [b] For 12:28-34 see parallel Matt. 22:34-40, 46 [c] Deut. 6:4, 5 [d] Lev. 19:18

discouraging to married couples who deeply love each other. Yet people will know their loved ones in heaven (see 8:11; Luke 9:30, 33).

12:26-27 The Lord is a covenant-keeping God, keeping his covenants with **Abraham ... Isaac, and ... Jacob**. And he is the God **of the living**. Abraham therefore continues to exist and to enjoy the blessings of God's covenant (see Rom. 8:35-39), and hence will also be raised from the dead.

12:28-31 love the Lord your God. This command (see Deut. 6:4-5) expresses the idea of total devotion

to God. It includes the duty to obey the rest of God's commandments (see Matt. 5:16-20). "Heart," "soul," and "mind" together refer to the whole person. **love your neighbor as yourself**. See Lev. 19:18, 34; Rom. 13:8-10; Gal. 5:14; 1 John 4:10-11.

12:34 Jesus declared that the scribe who had questioned him (v. 28) was **not far from the kingdom of God**. Among the key truths the scribe didn't understand were Jesus' identity as the beloved Son (9:7), as the one to be confessed (8:38), and as the one who would die on his behalf (10:45; see 12:35-37).

Whose Son Is the Christ?

[35][a]And as Jesus taught in the temple, he said, "How can the scribes say that the Christ is the son of David? [36]David himself, in the Holy Spirit, declared,

[b]" 'The Lord said to my Lord,

"Sit at my right hand,

until I put your enemies under your feet." '

[37]David himself calls him Lord. So how is he his son?" And the great throng heard him gladly.

Beware of the Scribes

[38][c]And in his teaching he said, "Beware of the scribes, who like to walk around in long robes and like greetings in the marketplaces [39]and have the best seats in the synagogues and the places of honor at feasts, [40]who devour widows' houses and for a pretense make long prayers. They will receive the greater condemnation."

The Widow's Offering

[41][d]And he sat down opposite the treasury and watched the people putting money into the offering box. Many rich people put in large sums. [42]And a poor widow came and put in two small copper coins, which make

---

[a] For 12:35-37 see parallels Matt. 22:41-45; Luke 20:41-44 [b] Ps. 110:1 [c] For 12:38-40 see parallels Matt. 23:1, 2, 5-7; Luke 20:45, 46 [d] For 12:41-44 see parallel Luke 21:1-4

....

12:35-37 While in the **temple**, Jesus publicly raises a question: who is the Messiah of God? Is he the **son** of David or the **Lord** of David? Jesus' point is not to deny that the Messiah is a descendant of David. The issue is that, in the quoted passage (Ps. 110:1-5), the Messiah is called the *Lord* of David. Jesus affirms that the Psalm was divinely inspired by the **Holy Spirit**. Jesus anticipates being exalted to the **right hand** of God, and thus he far transcends any expectation of a merely political, Davidic messiah.

12:38 scribes. Experts in handling written documents.

12:42-44 The **small copper coins** were worth about 1/128 of a denarius, which was a day's wage for a laborer.

a penny.[1] [43] And he called his disciples to him and said to them, "Truly, I say to you, this poor widow has put in more than all those who are contributing to the offering box. [44] For they all contributed out of their abundance, but she out of her poverty has put in everything she had, all she had to live on."

Jesus Foretells Destruction of the Temple

13 [a]And as he came out of the temple, one of his disciples said to him, "Look, Teacher, what wonderful stones and what wonderful buildings!" [2] And Jesus said to him, "Do you see these great buildings? There will not be left here one stone upon another that will not be thrown down."

Signs of the End of the Age

[3] And as he sat on the Mount of Olives opposite the temple, Peter and James and John and Andrew asked him privately, [4] "Tell us, when will these things be, and what will be the sign when all these things are about to be accomplished?" [5] And Jesus began to say to them, "See that no one leads you astray. [6] Many will come in my name, saying, 'I am he!' and they will lead many astray. [7] And when you hear of wars and rumors of wars, do not be alarmed. This must take place, but the end is not yet. [8] For nation will rise

---

[1] Greek *two lepta*, which make a *kodrantes*; a *kodrantes* (Latin *quadrans*) was a Roman copper coin worth about 1/64 of a *denarius* (which was a day's wage for a laborer) [a] For 13:1-37 see parallels Matt. 24:1-51; Luke 21:5-36

....

13:1 Herod the Great expanded the second **temple** to about double the size of Solomon's temple.

13:2 The temple would be destroyed because of its misuse by the leaders (see 12:9). **not . . . one stone upon another.** Titus, son of the emperor Vespasian, destroyed Jerusalem and the temple in AD 66–70.

13:3 The **Mount of Olives** (Olivet), with its spectacular view of the Temple Mount, stands just east of Jerusalem across the Kidron Valley. Jesus and his disciples regularly crossed over Olivet on their way from Jerusalem through Bethphage (Luke 19:29) to Bethany (John 11:1), which was on the mountain's eastern slope.

13:4–37 when will these things be, and what will be the sign? Jesus' answer deals primarily with the second part of the question, but he also addresses the timing of the coming events. The disciples assume that the destruction of the temple will coincide with the end of time, but Jesus corrects their thinking (vv. 7, 13). The destruction of Jerusalem (which came in AD 70) functions as a prophetic preview of the last judgment, which will occur when Jesus returns. God already knows about all these things, and the elect (vv. 20, 22, 27) will be preserved.

13:8 The symbolic language of **birth pains** describes the increase in frequency and duration of these end-time events.

against nation, and kingdom against kingdom. There will be earthquakes

in various places; there will be famines. These are but the beginning of the

birth pains.

[9] "But be on your guard. For they will deliver you over to councils, and

you will be beaten in synagogues, and you will stand before governors and

kings for my sake, to bear witness before them. [10] And the gospel must first

be proclaimed to all nations. [11] And when they bring you to trial and deliver

you over, do not be anxious beforehand what you are to say, but say whatever

is given you in that hour, for it is not you who speak, but the Holy Spirit.

[12] And brother will deliver brother over to death, and the father his child,

and children will rise against parents and have them put to death. [13] And

you will be hated by all for my name's sake. But the one who endures to

the end will be saved.

The Abomination of Desolation

[14] "But when you see the abomination of desolation standing where

he ought not to be (let the reader understand), then let those who are in

Judea flee to the mountains. [15] Let the one who is on the housetop not go

down, nor enter his house, to take anything out, [16] and let the one who

is in the field not turn back to take his cloak. [17] And alas for women who

are pregnant and for those who are nursing infants in those days! [18] Pray

that it may not happen in winter. [19] For in those days there will be such

13:14 The abomination of desolation (see Dan. 9:27; 11:31; 12:11) points to the Antichrist's ultimate desecration of God's temple (where he ought not to be; some understand this as a literal, rebuilt temple, and others understand it as the people of God; see 2 Thess. 2:1–12; 1 John 2:18). This event was anticipated in the destruction of the temple in Jerusalem. flee to the mountains. During the Jewish revolt (AD 67), Jesus' warning was fulfilled when Christians fled to the mountains of Pella.

13:19 Tribulation will occur in conjunction with the Antichrist's desecration of the temple (v. 14). It will involve the worst suffering since the beginning of the creation. The flight of Christians from Jerusalem in AD 67 pointed forward to this universal tribulation (see note on v. 14).

tribulation as has not been from the beginning of the creation that God created until now, and never will be. [20] And if the Lord had not cut short the days, no human being would be saved. But for the sake of the elect, whom he chose, he shortened the days. [21] And then if anyone says to you, 'Look, here is the Christ!' or 'Look, there he is!' do not believe it. [22] For false christs and false prophets will arise and perform signs and wonders, to lead astray, if possible, the elect. [23] But be on guard; I have told you all things beforehand.

The Coming of the Son of Man

[24] "But in those days, after that tribulation, the sun will be darkened, and the moon will not give its light, [25] and the stars will be falling from heaven, and the powers in the heavens will be shaken. [26] And then they will see the Son of Man coming in clouds with great power and glory. [27] And then he will send out the angels and gather his elect from the four winds, from the ends of the earth to the ends of heaven.

The Lesson of the Fig Tree

[28] "From the fig tree learn its lesson: as soon as its branch becomes tender and puts out its leaves, you know that summer is near. [29] So also,

---

13:20 The elect (see also vv. 22, 27) are those who have received God's gracious and undeserved call to salvation.

13:22 False prophets actually speak by demonic influence (1 John 4:3–4). One can test the spiritual influences that guide people by observing their doctrine and conduct. Unlike Scripture, **signs and wonders** are not clear indicators of God's presence (cf. the actions of the Antichrist in 2 Thess. 2:7–12). Jesus' remark that even **the elect** could be led astray emphasizes the stunning character of the false prophets' miracles. But God will protect his own, so that they will not believe in a false messiah or prophet.

13:24–26 After that tribulation clearly sets the further statements of Jesus apart from the preceding verses. **sun . . . moon . . . stars.** Jesus now describes cosmic events that will precede the **coming** of the **Son of Man.**

13:28–29 Some have understood **fig tree** here as a symbol for the nation of Israel (see note on 11:13–14), but it is more likely that in this case Jesus is just using a familiar event in nature as another illustration: **when you see these things taking place, you know** that Christ will come soon. "These things" probably refers not to the events of 13:24–27 (for they *are* the end) but the events of vv. 5–23.

when you see these things taking place, you know that he is near, at the very gates. [30] Truly, I say to you, this generation will not pass away until all these things take place. [31] Heaven and earth will pass away, but my words will not pass away.

No One Knows That Day or Hour

[32] "But concerning that day or that hour, no one knows, not even the angels in heaven, nor the Son, but only the Father. [33] Be on guard, keep awake.[1] For you do not know when the time will come. [34] It is like a man going on a journey, when he leaves home and puts his servants[2] in charge, each with his work, and commands the doorkeeper to stay awake. [35] Therefore stay awake—for you do not know when the master of the house will come, in the evening, or at midnight, or when the rooster crows,[3] or in the morning— [36] lest he come suddenly and find you asleep. [37] And what I say to you I say to all: Stay awake."

[1] Some manuscripts add *and pray* [2] Or *bondservants* [3] That is, the third watch of the night, between midnight and 3 A.M.

13:30 this generation will not pass away until all these things take place. Several interpretations have been offered as to what "this generation" refers to: (1) the disciples who were alive when Jesus was speaking, with "all these things" referring to the beginning but not the completion of the sufferings described in Matthew 24:4–25; (2) Jesus' disciples who see the destruction of the temple in AD 70 and also those at the end of the age who see the events surrounding the "abomination of desolation" (Matt. 24:15); (3) people who display a certain quality, that is, either (a) "this generation of believers" throughout the entire present age, or (b) "this evil generation" that will remain until Christ returns (cf. Matt. 12:45; Luke 11:29); (4) the "generation" or "race" of the Jewish people, who will not pass away until Christ returns; or (5) the generation that is alive when the final period of great tribulation begins.

13:31 my words will not pass away. Jesus claims that his words are more enduring than creation itself. He made the same claim for the words of the OT (Matt. 5:18).

13:32 nor the Son. In his life on earth, Jesus learned things as other human beings learn them (see Luke 2:52; Heb. 5:8). Yet Jesus was also fully God. As God, he could know things that only God knows (see John 16:30; 21:17). Here he is apparently speaking in terms of his human nature (see Matt. 4:2; Luke 2:40; John 4:6), not exercising his omniscience.

13:33–37 This parable about **a man going on a journey** is similar to the parable of the wicked tenants (12:1–12). The sudden return of the **master of the house** corresponds to the sudden coming of the Son of Man (**find you asleep**, 13:36; see Luke 17:24–32).

The Plot to Kill Jesus

14 [a] It was now two days before the Passover and the Feast of Unleavened Bread. And the chief priests and the scribes were seeking how to arrest him by stealth and kill him, [2] for they said, "Not during the feast, lest there be an uproar from the people."

Jesus Anointed at Bethany

[3] [b] And while he was at Bethany in the house of Simon the leper,[1] as he was reclining at table, a woman came with an alabaster flask of ointment of pure nard, very costly, and she broke the flask and poured it over his head. [4] There were some who said to themselves indignantly, "Why was the ointment wasted like that? [5] For this ointment could have been sold for more than three hundred denarii[2] and given to the poor." And they scolded her. [6] But Jesus said, "Leave her alone. Why do you trouble her? She has done a beautiful thing to me. [7] For you always have the poor with you, and whenever you want, you can do good for them. But you will not always have me. [8] She has done what she could; she has anointed my body beforehand for burial. [9] And truly, I say to you, wherever the gospel is proclaimed in the whole world, what she has done will be told in memory of her."

[1] *Leprosy* was a term for several skin diseases; see Leviticus 13 [2] A *denarius* was a day's wage for a laborer [a] For 14:1, 2 see parallels Matt. 26:2-5; Luke 22:1, 2 [b] For 14:3-9 see parallels Matt. 26:6-13; John 12:1-8

14:1–16:8 Death and Resurrection in Jerusalem. The final three chapters of Mark tell of the final week of Jesus' earthly life: his betrayal, arrest, trial, death, and resurrection.

14:3–5 Bethany. A village about 2 miles (3.2 km) from Jerusalem on the eastern slope of the Mount of Olives. The sale of such **costly** oil would have yielded more than 300 days' wages of a laborer. This story is also reported in Matt. 26:6–13 and John 12:1–8, where the woman is identified as Mary, sister of Martha and Lazarus. The story in Luke 7:36–50 is a different event, occurring at a different time in Jesus' ministry, with a different woman, different actions, different critics, and a different response from Jesus.

14:6–9 anointed . . . beforehand for burial. With this remark, Jesus again predicts his death (cf. 8:31; 9:30–31; 10:33–34). **you always have the poor with you.** Believers should **do good** for the poor, without expecting to completely eradicate poverty in this age (cf. Deut. 15:11). The inclusion of this story in the written Gospels fulfills Jesus' prediction that the story would be told **wherever the gospel is proclaimed in the whole world.**

Judas to Betray Jesus

[10][a] Then Judas Iscariot, who was one of the twelve, went to the chief priests in order to betray him to them. [11] And when they heard it, they were glad and promised to give him money. And he sought an opportunity to betray him.

The Passover with the Disciples

[12][b] And on the first day of Unleavened Bread, when they sacrificed the Passover lamb, his disciples said to him, "Where will you have us go and prepare for you to eat the Passover?" [13] And he sent two of his disciples and said to them, "Go into the city, and a man carrying a jar of water will meet you. Follow him, [14] and wherever he enters, say to the master of the house, 'The Teacher says, Where is my guest room, where I may eat the Passover with my disciples?' [15] And he will show you a large upper room furnished and ready; there prepare for us." [16] And the disciples set out and went to the city and found it just as he had told them, and they prepared the Passover.

a For 14:10, 11 see parallels Matt. 26:14-16; Luke 22:3-6 b For 14:12-16 see parallels Matt. 26:17-19; Luke 22:7-13

14:10–11 The Jewish authorities were **glad** for the help of **Judas Iscariot**; he would be able to tell them where Jesus could be found when there were no crowds present. Mark, like Luke (Luke 22:5), simply says Judas was given **money** in exchange for betraying Jesus; Matthew records the exact amount: "thirty pieces of silver" (Matt. 26:15).

14:12 The first day of **Unleavened Bread** (Ex. 12:15, 18) could refer to either Nisan 14 or Nisan 15, and **Passover** lambs were apparently killed on both days, but here Mark is referring to Nisan 14 (Thursday).

(Nisan usually falls somewhere in March/April in the Gregorian calendar) The Passover lamb is to be eaten within the walls of Jerusalem. Preparations for the meal have to be made inconspicuously, since Jesus is already a marked target.

14:13 a man carrying a jar of water. Something one would expect a woman to be doing.

14:16 just as he had told them. Either Jesus had made prior arrangements with friends in Jerusalem in order to avoid the Jewish authorities, or the encounter was a miraculous work of God.

[17] [a]And when it was evening, he came with the twelve. [18] And as they were reclining at table and eating, Jesus said, "Truly, I say to you, one of you will betray me, one who is eating with me." [19] They began to be sorrowful and to say to him one after another, "Is it I?" [20] He said to them, "It is one of the twelve, one who is dipping bread into the dish with me. [21] For the Son of Man goes as it is written of him, but woe to that man by whom the Son of Man is betrayed! It would have been better for that man if he had not been born."

Institution of the Lord's Supper

[22] [b]And as they were eating, he took bread, and after blessing it broke it and gave it to them, and said, "Take; this is my body." [23] And he took a cup, and when he had given thanks he gave it to them, and they all drank of it. [24] And he said to them, "This is my blood of the[1] covenant, which is poured out for many. [25] Truly, I say to you, I will not drink again of

[1] Some manuscripts insert *new* [a] For 14:17-21 see parallel Matt. 26:20-24 [b] For 14:22-25 see parallels Matt. 26:26-29; Luke 22:18-20

14:17 After sunset, the Passover meal begins. The celebrants remember the beginning of Israel's deliverance from slavery, when the Lord brought judgment by killing the firstborn in every Egyptian house but "passed over" the Israelite houses where the blood of the Passover lamb had been applied (Ex. 12:7). Those who celebrate the Passover also look forward to the ultimate liberation (Ex. 12:42). From now on, Jesus' blood will protect from judgment those who take refuge in him (1 Cor. 5:7).

14:18 reclining at table. In formal dining, the host took the center seat at a U-shaped series of low tables. He was surrounded by the most honored guests on either side. The guests reclined with their heads toward the tables and their feet toward the wall. Despite intimate fellowship, Judas will **betray** his master (Ps. 41:9).

14:21 Jesus confirms that **the Son of Man goes as it is written** (see Ps. 55:13-14; Isa. 53:1-12; Dan. 9:25-26; Mark 8:31). **but woe to that man.** Even though the Scriptures have predicted that Jesus would suffer a substitutionary death, Judas is responsible for his evil deed. Scripture consistently affirms both God's sovereignty and human responsibility.

14:22 The expression This is my body has been interpreted in various ways throughout the history of the church. Roman Catholics believe that the bread and wine actually become the body and blood of Christ. Lutherans believe that the literal body and blood of Christ are present "in, with, and under" the bread and wine. Some Anglicans refer to the "real presence" of Christ in the bread and wine. Most other Protestants believe that the body and blood of Christ are not literally, physically present in the elements of the meal, but that Christ is present symbolically. Most would also add that Christ is present spiritually with and in those who receive the elements in faith.

14:23-24 he took a cup. Most likely the third of four cups in the Passover observance—the cup of blessing, or the cup of redemption. It corresponds to God's third promise in Ex. 6:6. The communion wine corresponds to the covenant-establishing, once-and-for-all shed blood of Jesus as atonement **for many** (Mark 10:45; cf. Ex. 24:8; Isa. 53:12; Jer. 31:31-34).

14:25 that day when I drink it new. Jesus is confident that his impending death will not prevent his celebration in the future **kingdom of God**.

the fruit of the vine until that day when I drink it new in the kingdom of God."

Jesus Foretells Peter's Denial

26 [a]And when they had sung a hymn, they went out to the Mount of Olives. **27** And Jesus said to them, "You will all fall away, for it is written, 'I will [b] strike the shepherd, and the sheep will be scattered.' **28** But after I am raised up, I will go before you to Galilee." **29** Peter said to him, "Even though they all fall away, I will not." **30** And Jesus said to him, "Truly, I tell you, this very night, before the rooster crows twice, you will deny me three times." **31** But he said emphatically, "If I must die with you, I will not deny you." And they all said the same.

Jesus Prays in Gethsemane

32 [c]And they went to a place called Gethsemane. And he said to his disciples, "Sit here while I pray." **33** And he took with him Peter and James and John, and began to be greatly distressed and troubled. **34** And he said to them, "My soul is very sorrowful, even to death. Remain here and watch."[1] **35** And going a little farther, he fell on the ground and prayed that, if it were possible, the hour might pass from him. **36** And he said, "Abba, Father, all

[1] Or *keep awake*; also verses 37, 38 [a] For 14:26-31 see parallel Matt. 26:30-35 [b] Zech. 13:7 [c] For 14:32-42 see parallels Matt. 26:36-46; Luke 22:39-46

14:26 hymn. Perhaps Psalms 113–118, or Psalm 136. **went out to the Mount of Olives.** Passover celebrants were to remain in Jerusalem for this night (Deut. 16:7), therefore Jesus did not return to Bethany.

14:27–28 strike the shepherd, and the sheep will be scattered. Knowing that his disciples will soon desert him (see v. 50), Jesus quotes Zech. 13:7. The striking of the shepherd occurs in order to purify the people (Zech. 13:1, 7, 9). Jesus is confident that, though his flock will soon desert him, he will once again gather them (**after I am raised up**; see Mark 16:7). It is unclear why Jesus chooses **Galilee** (the home region of the disciples) as the place for this post-resurrection gathering. Perhaps it is so that the disciples will not expect a revolutionary event in Jerusalem (see Acts 1:6).

14:30 before the rooster crows twice. Each morning, roosters would crow a number of times separated by a few minutes. Jesus here specifies the first two individual crowings (see v. 72). Matthew, Luke, and John, however, refer to the entire time of several crowings.

14:32 Gethsemane means "oil press," indicating a garden area on the Mount of Olives where olive oil was prepared.

14:36 The cup is symbolic language for the wrath of

things are possible for you. Remove this cup from me. Yet not what I will, but what you will." **37** And he came and found them sleeping, and he said to Peter, "Simon, are you asleep? Could you not watch one hour? **38** Watch and pray that you may not enter into temptation. The spirit indeed is willing, but the flesh is weak." **39** And again he went away and prayed, saying the same words. **40** And again he came and found them sleeping, for their eyes were very heavy, and they did not know what to answer him. **41** And he came the third time and said to them, "Are you still sleeping and taking your rest? It is enough; the hour has come. The Son of Man is betrayed into the hands of sinners. **42** Rise, let us be going; see, my betrayer is at hand."

Betrayal and Arrest of Jesus

43 *a* And immediately, while he was still speaking, Judas came, one of the twelve, and with him a crowd with swords and clubs, from the chief priests and the scribes and the elders. **44** Now the betrayer had given them a sign, saying, "The one I will kiss is the man. Seize him and lead him away under guard." **45** And when he came, he went up to him at once and said, "Rabbi!" And he kissed him. **46** And they laid hands on him and seized him.

a For 14:43-50 see parallels Matt. 26:47-56; Luke 22:47-53; John 18:3-11

God, which he would pour out on sinners in righteous judgment. In this time of trial, Jesus entrusts himself into the hands of his **Father**. **Abba** was the word used by Jewish children for their earthly fathers. However, since the term in both Aramaic and Greek was also used by adults to address their fathers, the claim that "Abba" meant "Daddy" is misleading.

14:38 The spirit indeed is willing is a reference not to the Holy Spirit but to the disciples' human spirits. They desired to follow Jesus and be faithful (see v. 31), but quickly gave in to physical fatigue: **the flesh is weak**.

14:39 Saying the same words does not mean the "empty phrases" that Jesus had taught against

(Matt. 6:7). This was earnest repetition expressing the deep longing of his heart. For repetition in prayer, cf. Ps. 136:1-26; Isa. 6:3; 2 Cor. 12:8.

14:41 It is enough may mean: (1) enough prayer and wrestling with God—it is settled, and Jesus is going to the cross; (2) enough time—the end has come; or (3) enough sleep—it is time for the disciples to awake. **The hour** refers here to the time of Jesus' death and of his bearing divine judgment (as in vv. 35–36).

14:43–46 Armed temple officials, employed by the Jewish leaders, arrest Jesus (vv. 46, 53). As a traitor, **Judas** misuses familiar actions of respect and friendship: he calls Jesus **Rabbi** and greets him with a **kiss**.

[47] But one of those who stood by drew his sword and struck the servant[1] of the high priest and cut off his ear. [48] And Jesus said to them, "Have you come out as against a robber, with swords and clubs to capture me? [49] Day after day I was with you in the temple teaching, and you did not seize me. But let the Scriptures be fulfilled." [50] And they all left him and fled.

A Young Man Flees

[51] And a young man followed him, with nothing but a linen cloth about his body. And they seized him, [52] but he left the linen cloth and ran away naked.

Jesus Before the Council

[53] [a] And they led Jesus to the high priest. And all the chief priests and the elders and the scribes came together. [54] And Peter had followed him at a distance, right into the courtyard of the high priest. And he was sitting with the guards and warming himself at the fire. [55] Now the chief priests and the whole council[2] were seeking testimony against Jesus to put him to death, but they found none. [56] For many bore false witness against him, but their testimony did not agree. [57] And some stood up and bore false witness against him, saying, [58] "We heard him say, 'I will destroy this temple that is made with hands, and in three days I will build another, not made with hands.'" [59] Yet even about this their testimony did not agree. [60] And the high

---

[1] Or bondservant [2] Greek Sanhedrin [a] For 14:53-65 see parallel Matt. 26:57-68

14:47 cut off his ear. Peter (cf. John 18:10) probably intended to kill the soldier with a lethal blow to the head, but the servant only lost an ear. Luke adds that Jesus immediately healed the ear (Luke 22:51).

14:50 they all left him. See note on vv. 27–28.

14:52 he left the linen cloth. This incident is recorded only in Mark's Gospel. This has led many to think that Mark himself, the author of this Gospel, was this young man, but that out of modesty he did not include his own name.

14:53 Before daybreak on Friday, Nisan 15, Jesus is brought before the **high priest** Caiaphas and the Sanhedrin, which consisted of prominent Sadducees and Pharisees.

14:56 The **testimony** of the many witnesses **did not agree** and thus it could not be used in a formal charge against Jesus (see Deut. 17:6).

14:58 Jesus never said that *he* would **destroy** the temple (see John 2:19). He is innocent of this charge, as the high priest is surely aware.

priest stood up in the midst and asked Jesus, "Have you no answer to make? What is it that these men testify against you?"[1] [61] But he remained silent and made no answer. Again the high priest asked him, "Are you the Christ, the Son of the Blessed?" [62] And Jesus said, "I am, and you will see the Son of Man seated at the right hand of Power, and coming with the clouds of heaven." [63] And the high priest tore his garments and said, "What further witnesses do we need? [64] You have heard his blasphemy. What is your decision?" And they all condemned him as deserving death. [65] And some began to spit on him and to cover his face and to strike him, saying to him, "Prophesy!" And the guards received him with blows.

Peter Denies Jesus

[66] [a]And as Peter was below in the courtyard, one of the servant girls of the high priest came, [67] and seeing Peter warming himself, she looked at him and said, "You also were with the Nazarene, Jesus." [68] But he denied it, saying, "I neither know nor understand what you mean." And he went out into the gateway[2] and the rooster crowed.[3] [69] And the servant girl saw him and began again to say to the bystanders, "This man is one of them." [70] But again he denied it. And after a little while the bystanders again said to Peter, "Certainly you are one of them, for you are a Galilean." [71] But he began to invoke a curse on himself and to swear, "I do not know this man of whom you speak." [72] And immediately the rooster crowed a second time. And Peter

---

[1] Or Have you no answer to what these men testify against you? [2] Or forecourt [3] Some manuscripts omit and the rooster crowed [a] For 14:66-72 see parallels Matt. 26:69-75; Luke 22:55-62; John 18:16-18, 25-27

14:61–62 Are you the Christ, the Son of the Blessed? Jesus answers I am. He then claims to be the one who fulfills messianic prophecies from Ps. 110:1 and Dan. 7:13–14.

14:64 Jesus' statement (v. 62) is considered **blasphemy** because he claims to be the Son of God, with an exalted position at the right hand of God.

14:65 and to strike him. Mistreatment follows the verdict of v. 64. See Isa. 50:6; 53:2–3. Only the Roman authorities can carry out a death sentence (see note on Mark 15:1), so Jesus has to be taken to Pilate.

14:72 the rooster crowed a second time. See note on v. 30.

remembered how Jesus had said to him, "Before the rooster crows twice, you will deny me three times." And he broke down and wept.[1]

Jesus Delivered to Pilate

15 And as soon as it was morning, the chief priests held a consultation with the elders and scribes and the whole council. And they bound Jesus and led him away and delivered him over to Pilate. [2][a] And Pilate asked him, "Are you the King of the Jews?" And he answered him, "You have said so." [3] And the chief priests accused him of many things. [4] And Pilate again asked him, "Have you no answer to make? See how many charges they bring against you." [5] But Jesus made no further answer, so that Pilate was amazed.

Pilate Delivers Jesus to Be Crucified

[6][b] Now at the feast he used to release for them one prisoner for whom they asked. [7] And among the rebels in prison, who had committed murder in the insurrection, there was a man called Barabbas. [8] And the crowd came up and began to ask Pilate to do as he usually did for them. [9] And he answered them, saying, "Do you want me to release for you the King of the Jews?" [10] For he perceived that it was out of envy that the chief priests had delivered him up. [11] But the chief priests stirred up the crowd to have him release for them Barabbas

---

[1] Or *And when he had thought about it, he wept* [a] For 15:2-5 see parallels Matt. 27:11-14; Luke 23:1-3; John 18:28-38
[b] For 15:6-15 see parallels Matt. 27:15-26; Luke 23:18-25; John 18:39, 40; 19:16

. . . .

15:1 The whole council is the Sanhedrin. It did not have the right to execute a person. That right was reserved for Roman authorities, especially when dealing with popular figures. **Pilate** was temporarily in Jerusalem "to keep the peace" during the Passover. The Jewish authorities did not want to be busy with the case during the festive Passover day.

15:2 When they brought Jesus to **Pilate**, the Jewish authorities did not accuse him of blasphemy, a religious crime that would have made no difference to Pilate. Rather, they accused him of claiming to be **King of the Jews**. This was a direct challenge to Caesar's rule, and thus was a capital crime.

15:5 No further answer fulfills Isa. 53:7.

15:6–7 release . . . one prisoner. . . . Barabbas. A notorious criminal who had committed robbery, treason, and murder (Mark 15:7; Luke 23:18–19). He may have belonged to one of the rural guerilla bands that attacked Romans and wealthy Jews, making him popular with the common people.

15:11–13 release . . . Barabbas instead. Ironically, Pilate will free a man convicted of rebellion against

instead. [12] And Pilate again said to them, "Then what shall I do with the man

you call the King of the Jews?" [13] And they cried out again, "Crucify him."

[14] And Pilate said to them, "Why? What evil has he done?" But they shouted all

the more, "Crucify him." [15] So Pilate, wishing to satisfy the crowd, released for

them Barabbas, and having scourged[1] Jesus, he delivered him to be crucified.

Jesus Is Mocked

[16] [a] And the soldiers led him away inside the palace (that is, the governor's

headquarters),[2] and they called together the whole battalion.[3] [17] And they

clothed him in a purple cloak, and twisting together a crown of thorns,

they put it on him. [18] And they began to salute him, "Hail, King of the

Jews!" [19] And they were striking his head with a reed and spitting on him

and kneeling down in homage to him. [20] And when they had mocked him,

they stripped him of the purple cloak and put his own clothes on him. And

they led him out to crucify him.

The Crucifixion

[21] And they compelled a passerby, Simon of Cyrene, who was coming

in from the country, the father of Alexander and Rufus, to carry his cross.

---

[1] A Roman judicial penalty, consisting of a severe beating with a multi-lashed whip containing embedded pieces of bone and metal [2] Greek *the praetorium* [3] Greek *cohort*; a tenth of a Roman legion, usually about 600 men [a] For 15:16-20 see parallels Matt. 27:27-31; John 19:2, 3

Rome instead of a righteous man who has not spoken against Rome.

15:14 What evil has he done? See Isa. 53:9; Acts 3:13. By presenting evidence favorable to Jesus, Pilate tried to make the Jewish authorities solely responsible for his death. The fact remains, however, that Jesus' death occurred under Pilate's jurisdiction.

15:15 Pilate condemned Jesus to crucifixion, which was the means of executing criminals convicted of high treason. **having scourged Jesus.** Scourging, by itself, could lead to death.

15:16–19 The **governor's headquarters** has long been identified with the Antonia Fortress on the northwest corner of the Temple Mount. This large fortress allowed immediate access to the temple to stop any disturbance. However, many scholars believe that the Palace of Herod the Great would have afforded better accommodations for Pilate. This palace fortress, today called the Citadel, was at the western corner of the city. The presence of **the whole battalion** (about 600 men at full strength) means they are assuming that Jesus is a rebel against Rome (**King of the Jews**).

15:21 According to both Jewish and Roman custom, Jesus had to be taken outside the city walls to be crucified. As allowed by Roman law, **Simon of Cyrene** was forced to **carry** Jesus' **cross**. Crucifixion

[22] [a]And they brought him to the place called Golgotha (which means Place of a Skull). [23] And they offered him wine mixed with myrrh, but he did not take it. [24] And they crucified him and divided his garments among them, casting lots for them, to decide what each should take. [25] And it was the third hour[1] when they crucified him. [26] And the inscription of the charge against him read, "The King of the Jews." [27] And with him they crucified two robbers, one on his right and one on his left.[2] [29] And those who passed by derided him, wagging their heads and saying, "Aha! You who would destroy the temple and rebuild it in three days, [30] save yourself, and come down from the cross!" [31] So also the chief priests with the scribes mocked him to one another, saying, "He saved others; he cannot save himself. [32] Let the Christ, the King of Israel, come down now from the cross that we may see and believe." Those who were crucified with him also reviled him.

---

[1] That is, 9 A.M. [2] Some manuscripts insert verse 28: And the Scripture was fulfilled that says, "He was numbered with the transgressors" [a] For 15:22-38 see parallels Matt. 27:33-38; Luke 23:32-38, 44-46; John 19:17-19, 23, 24, 28-30

was the final public deterrent to warn people not to rebel against Rome. **Alexander and Rufus** may have been believers known in the early church at the time that Mark wrote his Gospel.

15:23 Wine mixed with myrrh is intended to have a mildly numbing effect.

15:24 And they crucified him. Jesus' hands were nailed above the wrist on the horizontal beam, and his feet were placed with one above the other and then nailed to the vertical beam. **Casting lots** fulfilled the prophecy in Ps. 22:18.

15:25 it was the third hour. John says "about the sixth hour," but he was not trying to give the exact time. The time references should not be seen as contradictory.

15:26 The inscription of the charge against him was

posted above Jesus' head, so that all could see why he was so shamefully executed. The inscription, **King of the Jews**, portrayed Jesus as a political rebel. This allowed Pilate to justify his actions. It also angered the Jewish authorities, who would never have claimed him as their king (John 19:19-22; cf. Mark 15:10).

15:27 The two robbers crucified with Jesus fulfill the prophecy of Isa. 53:12. Luke alone records that, sometime later, one of the two robbers repented and expressed faith in Jesus (Luke 23:39-43).

15:29-31 Because it was Passover, many **passed by** the place of Christ's crucifixion. **wagging their heads.** See Ps. 22:7-8. **You who would destroy the temple.** See note on Mark 14:58. Jesus appeared to have been silenced and divinely condemned for his blasphemy (see Deut. 21:23).

The Death of Jesus

33 And when the sixth hour[1] had come, there was darkness over the whole land until the ninth hour.[2] **34** And at the ninth hour Jesus cried with a loud voice, [a] "Eloi, Eloi, lema sabachthani?" which means, "My God, my God, why have you forsaken me?" **35** And some of the bystanders hearing it said, "Behold, he is calling Elijah." **36** And someone ran and filled a sponge with sour wine, put it on a reed and gave it to him to drink, saying, "Wait, let us see whether Elijah will come to take him down." **37** And Jesus uttered a loud cry and breathed his last. **38** And the curtain of the temple was torn in two, from top to bottom. **39** [b] And when the centurion, who stood facing him, saw that in this way he[3] breathed his last, he said, "Truly this man was the Son[4] of God!"

40 There were also women looking on from a distance, among whom were Mary Magdalene, and Mary the mother of James the younger and of Joses, and Salome. **41** When he was in Galilee, they followed him and ministered to him, and there were also many other women who came up with him to Jerusalem.

[1] That is, noon [2] That is, 3 P.M. [3] Some manuscripts insert *cried out and* [4] Or *a son* [a] Ps. 22:1 [b] For 15:39-41 see parallels Matt. 27:54-56; Luke 23:47, 49

15:33 Between noon and 3:00 p.m. there was **darkness**. This sign from God was not a solar eclipse. Darkness represents lament (Amos 8:9–10) and divine judgment.

15:34 My God, my God, why have you forsaken me? Jesus utters the opening words of Psalm 22. He expresses his immense pain at being abandoned by God, which he suffers as a substitute for sinful mankind. Yet the following verses of Psalm 22 also anticipate divine intervention on his behalf (cf. Heb. 5:7–9). Jesus knows why he is experiencing God-forsakenness, just as he knows his death will not be the end of his story.

15:35 he is calling Elijah. Bystanders misunderstand him as calling for the prophet.

15:36 sour wine. This "wine vinegar" was the ordinary wine soldiers drank. Giving him a drink would keep him alive and continue his suffering.

15:37 The final **loud cry** is probably the cry of victory, "It is finished" (John 19:30). In Mark's account, once Jesus dies, all mocking ceases. Subsequently, only the voices of the respectful (the centurion) and the mourners are heard. Jesus died around the time of the daily afternoon sacrifice in the temple.

15:38 The inner **curtain of the temple was torn in two, from top to bottom**, removing the separation between the Holy Place and the Most Holy Place (see Heb. 10:19–20). Access to God is now provided by the unique sacrifice of Jesus, making the temple sacrifices obsolete.

15:39 The **centurion** has observed the death of many crucified criminals. He recognizes correctly that Jesus is **the Son of God**.

15:40 women looking on. These women are singled out because of their role in the resurrection account. **Mary Magdalene.** She was from Magdala,

Jesus Is Buried

[42] [a]And when evening had come, since it was the day of Preparation, that is, the day before the Sabbath, [43] Joseph of Arimathea, a respected member of the council, who was also himself looking for the kingdom of God, took courage and went to Pilate and asked for the body of Jesus. [44] Pilate was surprised to hear that he should have already died.[1] And summoning the centurion, he asked him whether he was already dead. [45] And when he learned from the centurion that he was dead, he granted the corpse to Joseph. [46] And Joseph[2] bought a linen shroud, and taking him down, wrapped him in the linen shroud and laid him in a tomb that had been cut out of the rock. And he rolled a stone against the entrance of the tomb. [47] Mary Magdalene and Mary the mother of Joses saw where he was laid.

The Resurrection

16 [b]When the Sabbath was past, Mary Magdalene, Mary the mother of James, and Salome bought spices, so that they might go and anoint him. [2] And very early on the first day of the week, when the sun had risen, they

---

[1] Or *Pilate wondered whether he had already died*   [2] Greek *he*   [a] For 15:42-47 see parallels Matt. 27:57-61; Luke 23:50-56; John 19:38-42   [b] For 16:1-8 see parallels Matt. 28:1-8; Luke 24:1-10; John 20:1

---

on the western shore of Galilee. Later writers in church history connected Mary Magdalene to the sinful woman of 7:37, calling her a former prostitute. Jesus healed Mary of demonic possession, and she gratefully followed him to the foot of the cross and the empty tomb.

15:42 Deuteronomy 21:23 says that a corpse should be buried on the day of death (taking priority over Passover; see John 19:40). The **day of Preparation** is the day before the Sabbath.

15:43 **Joseph of Arimathea** courageously intended to bury Jesus before the Sabbath began at sundown (Nisan 16). Matthew 27:57 calls him "a disciple of Jesus."

15:46 Joseph wrapped the body of Jesus in a **linen shroud** and placed it **in a tomb . . . cut out of the rock**. Rock-cut tombs were expensive since they required

extensive excavation. This tomb would most probably have been Joseph of Arimathea's family tomb. After a body had decayed, its bones were removed and piled elsewhere in the tomb or reburied in an ossuary, a specially designed box which held one or two bodies. The two main locations where it is thought that Jesus may have been buried are the Church of the Holy Sepulchre and the Garden Tomb. Both of these were rock-cut tombs with rolling stone doors. Both would have been outside the first-century city walls. Early church tradition strongly favors the Holy Sepulchre site. The area around the Garden Tomb consists largely of tombs from OT times.

16:1-2 Once the **Sabbath** is over (at sundown on Saturday evening), the women can buy oils for embalming of the corpse after sunrise on Sunday

went to the tomb. [3] And they were saying to one another, "Who will roll away

the stone for us from the entrance of the tomb?" [4] And looking up, they saw

that the stone had been rolled back—it was very large. [5] And entering the

tomb, they saw a young man sitting on the right side, dressed in a white

robe, and they were alarmed. [6] And he said to them, "Do not be alarmed. You

seek Jesus of Nazareth, who was crucified. He has risen; he is not here. See

the place where they laid him. [7] But go, tell his disciples and Peter that he

is going before you to Galilee. There you will see him, just as he told you."

[8] And they went out and fled from the tomb, for trembling and astonishment

had seized them, and they said nothing to anyone, for they were afraid.

[SOME OF THE EARLIEST MANUSCRIPTS DO NOT INCLUDE 16:9–20.][1]

Jesus Appears to Mary Magdalene

[9] [[Now when he rose early on the first day of the week, he appeared

first to Mary Magdalene, from whom he had cast out seven demons. [10] She

went and told those who had been with him, as they mourned and wept.

[11] But when they heard that he was alive and had been seen by her, they

would not believe it.

[1] Some manuscripts end the book with 16:8; others include verses 9–20 immediately after verse 8. At least one manuscript inserts additional material after verse 14; some manuscripts include after verse 8 the following: *But they reported briefly to Peter and those with him all that they had been told. And after this, Jesus himself sent out by means of them, from east to west, the sacred and imperishable proclamation of eternal salvation.* These manuscripts then continue with verses 9–20

. . . .

morning (**the first day of the week**). This occurred on the "third day" (see 8:31; 10:34).

16:5 they saw a young man. An angel. Luke 24:4 and John 20:12 give additional information and say there were two angels, but Mark and Matthew mention only one (see Matt. 28:2–5).

16:7 go, tell his disciples. In NT times, the testimony of women as witnesses was not always believed, especially in a court of law. After the initial encounters with the risen Jesus in Jerusalem, **Galilee** again served as a place of preparation (as Jesus had predicted in 14:28). Jesus thus avoided the possibility

that the disciples might expect him to usher in a political, messianic kingdom in Jerusalem. However, see Acts 1:6.

16:8 they said nothing to anyone. Their silence would be only temporary (see Matt. 28:8).

16:9–20 "Longer Ending of Mark." Some ancient manuscripts of Mark's Gospel contain these verses and others do not. Early church fathers did not appear to know of these verses. Eusebius and Jerome state that this section is missing in most manuscripts available at their time. And some manuscripts that contain vv. 9–20 indicate that older

Jesus Appears to Two Disciples

[12] After these things he appeared in another form to two of them, as they were walking into the country. [13] And they went back and told the rest, but they did not believe them.

The Great Commission

[14] Afterward he appeared to the eleven themselves as they were reclining at table, and he rebuked them for their unbelief and hardness of heart, because they had not believed those who saw him after he had risen. [15] And he said to them, "Go into all the world and proclaim the gospel to the whole creation. [16] Whoever believes and is baptized will be saved, but whoever does not believe will be condemned. [17] And these signs will accompany those who believe: in my name they will cast out demons; they will speak in new tongues; [18] they will pick up serpents with their hands; and if they drink any deadly poison, it will not hurt them; they will lay their hands on the sick, and they will recover."

[19] So then the Lord Jesus, after he had spoken to them, was taken up into heaven and sat down at the right hand of God. [20] And they went out and preached everywhere, while the Lord worked with them and confirmed the message by accompanying signs.]]

manuscripts lack the section. As for the verses themselves, they contain various Greek words and expressions uncommon to Mark, and there are stylistic differences as well. Many think this shows vv. 9–20 to be a later addition. In summary, vv. 9–20 should be read with caution. As in many translations, the editors of the ESV have placed the section within brackets, showing their doubts as to whether it was originally part of what Mark wrote. Most of the content of these verses is found elsewhere in the NT, and no point of doctrine is affected by their absence or presence. Verse 18 does not command believers to **pick up serpents** or to drink **deadly poison**; it merely promises protection if such a thing were to occur (see Acts 28:3–4; James 5:13–16).

The Three Major Passion Predictions in Mark

Three times in Mark 8–10 Jesus predicts his death, the disciples fail to understand or to respond appropriately, and he then teaches them about discipleship.

Announcement of Jesus' Death	Failure on the Part of the Disciples	Jesus Teaches on Discipleship
Jesus will suffer, be rejected, killed, and will rise after three days (8:31)	Peter rebukes Jesus (8:32–33)	Jesus commands them to deny themselves, take up their cross, and follow him (8:33–9:1)
Jesus will be delivered, killed, and will rise after three days (9:30–31)	The disciples do not understand the saying and are afraid to ask him about it (9:32)	Jesus teaches that the first must be last and that those who receive children in his name receive him (9:33–50)
Jesus will be delivered, condemned, mocked, flogged, killed, and will rise after three days (10:33–34)	James and John ask that they may sit next to Jesus in his glory (10:35–37)	Jesus teaches that, to be great, they must become servants; to be first, they must become slaves; and that he came to serve by giving his life as a ransom for many (10:38–45)

The Synagogue and Jewish Worship

The Greek word "synagogue" means "congregation." By Jesus' time, synagogues were a fixture in Jewish life in Judea and Galilee and in foreign lands. They were particularly important in foreign lands, where Jewish exiles had first gone seven centuries earlier. Gathering for weekly Sabbath worship and for other major life events helped Jews preserve their faith. It also helped them pass on their faith to Gentiles, who were called "God fearers" (see Neh. 7:2; Acts 10:22). As Paul traveled throughout the Roman Empire, he proclaimed Jesus as the Messiah in local synagogues (Acts 13:13–42; 17:1–2).

Synagogues were led by lay elders, one of whom was the "ruler" (see Mark 5:22; Luke 8:41; Acts 18:8). He invited speakers (Acts 13:15), kept order (Luke 13:14), and oversaw services. Sabbath worship services included singing, prayers, Scripture readings, a sermon on the Scriptures that had been read, and a closing blessing. Luke 4:16–27 reports Jesus reading and explaining Scripture at the synagogue in Nazareth, his hometown.

Synagogues were usually simple in design. They typically consisted of a single room with bench seating along the wall. Some congregations did not have a separate building, so they met in rooms in private homes. Where there were too few Jews to form a congregation, people also met to pray at outdoor locations (see Acts 16:13).

This illustration is based on the excavated synagogue in Gamla, c. 6 miles (9 km) northeast of the Sea of Galilee. It is thought to be one of the oldest in Israel. It would be similar to the synagogues Jesus visited in Capernaum and other cities (Matt. 9:35; Mark 1:39; Luke 4:16, 44).

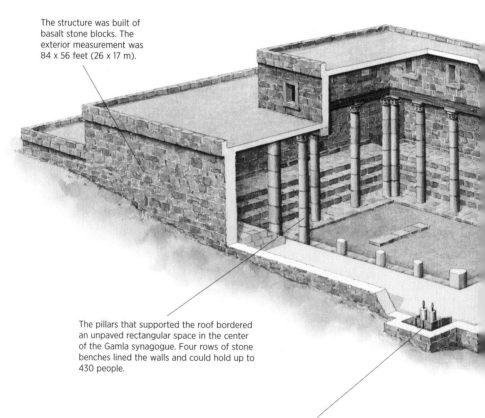

The structure was built of basalt stone blocks. The exterior measurement was 84 x 56 feet (26 x 17 m).

The pillars that supported the roof bordered an unpaved rectangular space in the center of the Gamla synagogue. Four rows of stone benches lined the walls and could hold up to 430 people.

A closet held scrolls of the Scriptures.

Synagogue Architectural Plan

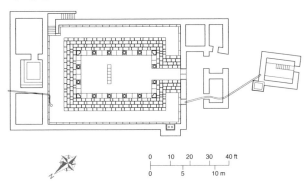

0 10 20 30 40 ft
0   5   10 m

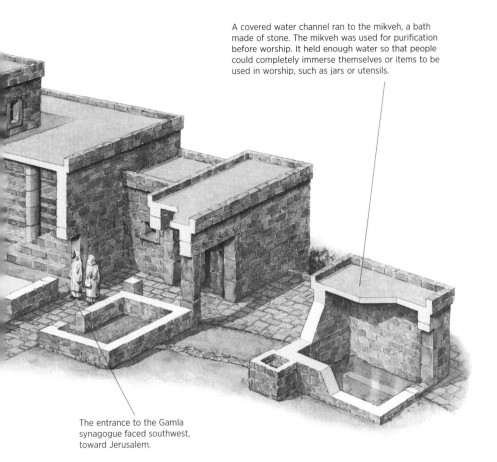

A covered water channel ran to the mikveh, a bath made of stone. The mikveh was used for purification before worship. It held enough water so that people could completely immerse themselves or items to be used in worship, such as jars or utensils.

The entrance to the Gamla synagogue faced southwest, toward Jerusalem.

GLOSSARY

Anoint

In Scripture, to pour oil (usually olive oil) on someone or something to set the person or thing apart for a special purpose. (The Hebrew word *Messiah* and its Greek equivalent *Christ* both mean "anointed one.") In Mark 16:1, the women anoint Jesus' body as part of the embalming process.

Baptize

Literally "to immerse" or "to wash." Refers to the Christian practice of immersing a new believer in water as an outward sign of the inward reality of regeneration. This regeneration is the work of the Holy Spirit (see John 3:5, 8; Titus 3:5). Considerable disagreement exists as to the method of baptism (i.e., sprinkling vs. immersion) and who may be baptized (i.e., believers only vs. believers and their infant children).

Blasphemy

Any speech, writing, or action that slanders God. In the OT, the penalty for blasphemy was death. (Lev. 24:16).

Christ's Second Coming

The OT looked forward to the coming of the Messiah, the Christ. Surprisingly, when the Christ came and the kingdom of God dawned, this new age brought forgiveness of sins yet did not bring full redemption of the body and the physical world. Sin and suffering remained. Thus the Christ has already come once, decisively inaugurating the new world longed for in the OT, and the Christ will come again, bringing to full and final fulfillment the redemption of the cosmos and the eradication of all sin and suffering.

Crucifixion

A means of execution in which the person was fastened, by ropes or nails, to a crossbeam that was then raised and attached to a vertical beam, forming a cross (the root meaning of "crucifixion"). The process was designed to maximize pain and humiliation, and to serve as a deterrent for other potential offenders. Jesus suffered this form of execution, not for any offense he had committed (Heb. 4:15) but as the atoning sacrifice for all who would believe in him (Mark 10:45; John 3:16).

Demon

An evil spirit that can inhabit ("possess") a human being and influence him or her to carry out its will. Demons were rebel angels, originally created by God, and they are always limited by God. Jesus and his followers cast out many demons, demonstrating the coming of the kingdom of God and Jesus' superiority. All demons will one day be destroyed along with Satan (Matt. 25:41; Rev. 20:10).

Discipleship

Submitting to the teachings of another and following that person's way of life. In the NT, disciples were those who submitted themselves to the teaching of Jesus, especially the twelve men who traveled and lived with Jesus during his earthly ministry.

Exodus, the

The departure of the people of Israel from Egypt and their journey to Mount Sinai under Moses' leadership (Exodus 1–19; Numbers 33). The exodus demonstrated God's power and providence for his people, who had been enslaved by the Egyptians. The annual festival of Passover commemorates God's final plague upon the Egyptians, resulting in Israel's release from Egypt. Mark 1:1–13 makes several allusions to the exodus to highlight the importance of Jesus' coming and work.

Faith

Trust in or reliance upon something or someone for solid reasons, yielding certainty. Salvation, which is purely a work of God's grace, can be received only through faith in Jesus Christ (Rom. 5:2; Eph. 2:8–9). The writer of Hebrews calls on believers to emulate those who lived godly lives by faith (Hebrews 11).

Gentile

Anyone who is not Jewish. At times the NT uses the term "Greek" as a synonym for Gentile (e.g., 1 Cor. 1:22–23).

Grace

Unmerited favor, especially the free gift of salvation that God gives to believers through faith in Jesus Christ.

Herod the Great

Herod I, also known as Herod the Great, ruled Israel and Judah from 37–4 BC. He was not Roman by birth but had been appointed king of the Jews under the authority of Rome. He ruled firmly and at times ruthlessly, and was a master builder who not only restored the temple in Jerusalem but also built many theaters, cities, palaces, and fortresses.

Holy Spirit
One of the persons of the Trinity, and thus fully God. The Bible mentions several roles of the Holy Spirit, including convicting people of sin, bringing them to conversion, indwelling them and empowering them to live in Christlike righteousness and service, supporting them in times of trial, and enabling them to understand the Scriptures. The Holy Spirit was poured out at Pentecost in Acts 2 in fulfillment of Old Testament prophecy (e.g., Ezek. 36:26–27). The Spirit was vitally active in Jesus' life and ministry on earth (e.g., Mark 1:10).

Israel
Originally, another name given to Jacob (Gen. 32:28). Later applied to the nation formed by his descendants, then to the ten northern tribes of that nation, who rejected the anointed king and formed their own nation. In the NT, the name is applied to the church as the spiritual descendants of Abraham (e.g., Gal. 6:16).

Kingdom of God
The rule of God manifested in the long-awaited restoration of his people and indeed the whole world, in which God would reign under the glad submission of all people. When Jesus came two thousand years ago, he announced that the kingdom of God had arrived (Mark 1:15; Luke 17:20–21). Yet because of ongoing rebellion and rejection of Jesus and his rule, the kingdom still awaits its final consummation and fulfillment in Jesus' second coming (Mark 14:25). For this reason we pray for the kingdom to come (Matt. 6:10).

Law
When spelled with an initial capital letter, "Law" refers to the first five books of the Bible. The Law contains numerous commands of God to his people, including the Ten Commandments and instructions regarding worship, sacrifice, and life in Israel. The NT often uses "the law" (lower case) to refer to the entire body of precepts set forth in the books of the Law, and reinforced by the rest of the Bible.

Leper
A leper was someone suffering from leprosy, which was a term for a variety of related skin diseases, many of which were highly contagious. See Leviticus 13.

Lord's Supper
A meal of remembrance instituted by Jesus on the night of his betrayal. Christians are to observe this meal, also called Communion, in remembrance of Jesus' death. It consists of wine, symbolizing the new covenant in his blood, and bread, symbolizing his body, which was broken for his followers.

Messiah
Transliteration of a Hebrew word meaning "anointed one," the equivalent of the Greek word *Christ.* "Anointed one" signified kingship. The Messiah therefore came to mean the anticipated coming king who would liberate Israel once and for all and bring in the kingdom of God. Jesus affirmed that he was the Messiah sent from God (Matt. 16:16 –17; Mark 8:29–30).

Parable
A story that uses everyday imagery and activities to communicate a spiritual truth. Jesus often taught in parables.

Passover
An annual Israelite festival commemorating God's final plague on the Egyptians, which led to the exodus. In this final plague, the Lord "passed over" the houses of those who spread the blood of a lamb on the doorposts of their homes (Exodus 12). Those who did not obey this command suffered the death of their firstborn. Jesus is the final and true Passover lamb (1 Cor. 5:7).

Pharisee
A member of a popular religious party in NT times characterized by strict adherence to the law of Moses and also to extrabiblical Jewish traditions. The Pharisees were frequently criticized by Jesus for their hypocritical practices. The apostle Paul was a zealous Pharisee prior to his conversion.

Prophet
Someone who speaks authoritatively for God. When the NT refers to "the prophets," it is referring either to a specific group of OT books (e.g., Matt. 5:17; Luke 24:44), or, more generally, to those who spoke to God's people on behalf of God throughout the OT between the time of Moses and the close of the OT.

Resurrection
The impartation of restored life to a dead person. The NT teaches that Christians have already been resurrected spiritually (Eph. 2:5–6; Col. 3:1), but they have not yet been raised physically (2 Cor. 5:1–5). Physical resurrection will happen at the end of time, when both the righteous and the wicked will be resurrected, the former to eternal life and the latter to retributive judgment (John 5:29).

Sabbath
For Jews the Sabbath is Saturday, the seventh day of the week, a day of worship and rest (Gen. 2:2–3; Ex. 31:13–17). Christians meet for worship on Sunday, the day of Christ's resurrection (Acts 20:7), and regard Sunday, rather than Saturday, as their weekly day of rest. Believers also look forward to an eternal Sabbath rest, won for them by Jesus (Heb. 4:1–16).

Sacrifice
An offering to God, often to signify forgiveness of sin. The Law of Moses gave detailed instructions regarding various kinds of sacrifices.

Sanhedrin

Either a local Jewish tribunal ("council," Matt. 5:22; "courts," Matt. 10:17) or as in Mark 15, the supreme ecclesiastical court in Jerusalem (cf. Matt. 26:59). These Jewish leaders included elders, chief priests, and scribes.

Satan

A spiritual being whose name means "accuser." As the leader of all the demonic forces, he opposes God's rule and seeks to harm God's people and accuse them of wrongdoing. His power, however, is confined to the bounds that God has set for him, and one day he will be destroyed along with all his demons (Matt. 25:41; Rev. 20:10).

Sovereignty

Supreme and independent power and authority. Sovereignty over all things is a distinctive attribute of God (1 Tim. 6:15-16). He directs all things to carry out his purposes (Rom. 8:28-29).

Synagogue

In Jerusalem, worship took place at the temple. In cities other than Jerusalem, however, which had no temple, the synagogue (meaning "assembly") was the center of Jewish worship. Synagogues were located in most of the leading towns of Israel.

Ten Commandments

Also called the "ten words," these are the commands God gave to Moses on two stone tablets on Mount Sinai. Moses then brought these down to the people of Israel. These commandments were given to God's people after God redeemed them from Egyptian slavery, setting a pattern found throughout the Bible—God first shows mercy to his people, then calls them to live before him in integrity. Grace fuels obedience.

Temple

A special building set aside as holy because of God's presence there. Solomon built the first temple of the Lord in Jerusalem, to replace the portable tabernacle. This temple was later destroyed by the Babylonians, rebuilt, and then destroyed again by the Romans. Jesus is the true and final temple (John 2:18-22), and all those united to him become part of this temple too (Eph. 2:20-22).

Transfiguration

An event in the life of Jesus Christ in which his physical appearance was transfigured, that is, changed to reflect his heavenly glory.

Tribulation

Trial or difficulty. In Christian theology regarding the end times, many believe the NT teaches that there will be a final, climactic, and intensified "tribulation" just prior to Christ's second coming.

CONCORDANCE

ABLE
against itself, that house will not be **a** to stand. 3:25
he spoke the word to them, as they were **a** to hear it. 4:33
disciples to cast it out, and they were not **a**."...............9:18
name will be **a** soon afterward to speak evil of me.....9:39
Are you **a** to drink the cup that I drink, ...10:38
And they said to him, "We are **a**." 10:39

ADULTERY
sexual immorality, theft, murder, **a,**............................7:21
wife and marries another commits **a**...........................10:11
and marries another, she commits **a**."..........................10:12
'Do not murder, Do not commit **a,** 10:19

AFRAID
"Why are you so **a**? Have you still no faith?" 4:40
clothed and in his right mind, and they were **a**...........5:15
them and said, "Take heart; it is I. Do not be **a**."........6:50
not understand the saying, and were a to ask him. 9:32
were amazed, and those who followed were **a**. 10:32
we say, 'From man'?"—they were **a** of the people,.....11:32
and they said nothing to anyone, for they were **a**......16:8

AGE
up and began walking (for she was twelve years of **a**),..5:42
persecutions, and in the **a** to come eternal life. 10:30

ALARMED
of wars and rumors of wars, do not be **a**.....................13:7
in a white robe, and they were **a**....................................16:5
"Do not be **a**. You seek Jesus of 16:6

ALONE
He is blaspheming! Who can forgive sins but God **a**?" 2:7
And when he was **a**, those around him with the.........4:10
was out on the sea, and he was **a** on the land. 6:47
do you call me good? No one is good except God **a**.10:18
Jesus said, "Leave her **a**. Why do you trouble her?".... 14:6

AMAZED
And they were all **a**, so that they questioned...............1:27
so that they were all **a** and glorified God, saying, ...2:12
when they saw him, were greatly **a** and.........................9:15
And the disciples were **a** at his words. 10:24
they were **a**, and those who followed were...............10:32
made no further answer, so that Pilate was **a**..............15:5

ANGELS
and the **a** were ministering to him...................................1:13
in the glory of his Father with the holy **a**."...................8:38
are given in marriage, but are like **a** in heaven..........12:25
And then he will send out the **a** and gather his.........13:27
knows, not even the **a** in heaven, nor the Son,...........13:32

AUTHORITY
for he taught them as one who had **a,**...........................1:22
"What is this? A new teaching with **a**! 1:27
Son of Man has **a** on earth to forgive sins"..................2:10
and have **a** to cast out demons. 3:15
and gave them **a** over the unclean spirits........................6:7
great ones exercise **a** over them...................................10:42
"By what **a** are you doing these things, ...11:28
or who gave you this **a** to do them?"............................11:28

I will tell you by what **a** I do these things. 11:29
"Neither will I tell you by what **a** I do these 11:33

AWAKE
Be on guard, keep **a**. For you do not know 13:33
and commands the doorkeeper to stay **a**....................13:34
Therefore stay **a**—..13:35
And what I say to you I say to all: Stay **a**." 13:37

BAPTIZED
were going out to him and were being **b** by him...........1:5
I have **b** you with water, but he will baptize....................1:8
of Galilee and was **b** by John in the Jordan. 1:9
or to be **b** with the baptism with which I am..............10:38
baptized with the baptism with which I am **b**?"........10:38
with the baptism with which I am **b**, you will 10:39
with which I am baptized, you will be **b,**.....................10:39
Whoever believes and is **b** will be saved,....................16:16

BEGGED
And he **b** him earnestly not to send them out............. 5:10
and they **b** him, saying, "Send us to the pigs;..............5:12
with demons **b** him that he might be with him. 5:18
she **b** him to cast the demon out of her daughter.......7:26
and they **b** him to lay his hand on him. 7:32
to him a blind man and **b** him to touch him.................8:22

BEGINNING
The **b** of the gospel of Jesus Christ, ...1:1
But from the **b** of creation, 'God made them...............10:6
These are but the **b** of the birth pains. 13:8
as has not been from the **b** of the creation.................13:19

BELIEVE
of God is at hand; repent and **b** in the gospel." 1:15
ruler of the synagogue, "Do not fear, only **b**." 5:36
cried out and said, "I **b**; help my unbelief!"..................9:24
causes one of these little ones who **b** in me to...........9:42
b that you have received it, and it will be....................11:24
he will say, 'Why then did you not **b** him?' 11:31
is the Christ!' or 'Look, there he is!' do not **b** it. 13:21
now from the cross that we may see and **b**."..............15:32
and had been seen by her, they would not **b** it. 16:11
back and told the rest, but they did not **b** them........16:16
but whoever does not **b** will be condemned..............16:16
And these signs will accompany those who **b**:...........16:17

BLESSED
having **b** them, he said that these also should be 8:7
And he took them in his arms and **b** them,.................10:16
b is he who comes in the name of the Lord!...............11:9
b is the coming kingdom of our father David!............11:10
"Are you the Christ, the Son of the **b**?" 14:61

BLIND
brought to him a **b** man and begged him to...............8:22
And he took the **b** man by the hand and led him.......8:23
Bartimaeus, a **b** beggar, the son of Timaeus,............10:46
called the **b** man, saying to him, "Take heart............10:49
the **b** man said to him, "Rabbi, let me recover my 10:51

BOUND
for he had often been **b** with shackles and chains, ...5:4

had sent and seized John and **b** him in prison 6:17
they **b** Jesus and led him away and delivered him.......15:1

BROUGHT

at sundown they **b** to him all who were sick..................1:32
"Is a lamp **b** in to be put under a basket,....................4:21
b his head on a platter and gave it to the girl,..........6:28
And they **b** to him a man who was deaf and 7:32
some people **b** to him a blind man and begged 8:22
I **b** my son to you, for he has a spirit that makes........9:17
And they **b** the boy to him. And when the spirit 9:20
they **b** the colt to Jesus and threw their cloaks on 11:7
And they **b** one. And he said to them, ...12:16
And they **b** him to the place called Golgotha.............15:22

CAST

various diseases, and **c** out many demons. 1:34
and have authority to **c** out demons. 3:15
in parables, "How can Satan **c** out Satan? 3:23
they **c** out many demons and anointed with...............6:13
she begged him to **c** the demon out of her..................7:26
I asked your disciples to **c** it out, and they 9:18
And it has often **c** him into fire and into water,.........9:22
him privately, "Why could we not **c** it out?"...............9:28
from whom he had **c** out seven demons. 16:9
believe: in my name they will **c** out demons; 16:17

CHARGED

Jesus sternly **c** him and sent him away at once,...........1:43
he strictly **c** them that no one should know this,.......5:43
He **c** them to take nothing for their journey..................6:8
And Jesus **c** them to tell no one. 7:36
the more he **c** them, the more zealously they 7:36
And he strictly **c** them to tell no one about him. 8:30
he **c** them to tell no one what they had seen,..............9:9

CLEAN

said to him, "If you will, you can make me **c**." 1:40
touched him and said to him, "I will; be **c**."..................1:41
the leprosy left him, and he was made **c**....................1:42
(Thus he declared all foods **c**.)....................................7:19

CROSS

deny himself and take up his **c** and follow me.............8:34
the father of Alexander and Rufus, to carry his **c**. 15:21
save yourself, and come down from the **c**!" 15:30
come down now from the **c** that we may see and.....15:32

DEFILE

a person that by going into him can **d** him, ...7:15
that come out of a person are what **d** him." 7:15
goes into a person from outside cannot **d** him, ...7:18
things come from within, and they **d** a person." 7:23

DENY

let him **d** himself and take up his cross and follow 8:34
rooster crows twice, you will **d** me three times."......14:30
"If I must die with you, I will not **d** you."......................14:31
rooster crows twice, you will **d** me three times." 14:72

EARS

And he said, "He who has **e** to hear, let him hear." 4:9
If anyone has **e** to hear, let him hear."..........................4:23
he put his fingers into his **e**, and after spitting............7:33
And his **e** were opened, his tongue was..........................7:35
eyes do you not see, and having **e** do you not hear?..8:18

ELECT

But for the sake of the **e**, whom he chose, ...13:20
and wonders, to lead astray, if possible, the **e**...........13:22
angels and gather his **e** from the four winds, ...13:27

ELIJAH

But others said, "He is **E**."..6:15
told him, "John the Baptist; and others say, **E**; 8:28
And there appeared to them **E** with Moses,..................9:4
one for you and one for Moses and one for **E**." 9:5
do the scribes say that first **E** must come?".................9:11
to them, "**E** does come first to restore all things. 9:12
I tell you that **E** has come, and they did to him...........9:13

hearing it said, "Behold, he is calling **E**."......................15:35
us see whether **E** will come to take him down." 15:36

EVIL

within, out of the heart of man, come **e** thoughts,.......7:21
All these **e** things come from within,............................7:23
will be able soon afterward to speak **e** of me.............9:39
Pilate said to them, "Why, what **e** has he done?" 15:14

FAITH

when Jesus saw their **f**, he said to the paralytic, ... 2:5
"Why are you so afraid? Have you still no **f**?"............. 4:40
to her, "Daughter, your **f** has made you well;..............5:34
him, "Go your way; your **f** has made you well." 10:52
And Jesus answered them, "Have **f** in God................. 11:22

FOLLOW

"**f** me, and I will make you become 1:17
and he said to him, "**f** me." And he rose and 2:14
And he allowed no one to **f** him except Peter 5:37
deny himself and take up his cross and **f** me..............8:34
will have treasure in heaven; and come, **f** me." 10:21
carrying a jar of water will meet you. **f** him, ...14:13

FORGIVE

Who can **f** sins but God alone?" 2:7
the Son of Man has authority on earth to **f** sins"........ 2:10
And whenever you stand praying, **f**,...........................11:25
who is in heaven may **f** you your trespasses." 11:25

FRUIT

who hear the word and accept it and bear **f**,.............. 4:20
"May no one ever eat **f** from you again."......................11:14
to get from them some of the **f** of the vineyard. 12:2
I will not drink again of the **f** of the vine until...........14:25

GOOD

it lawful on the Sabbath to do **g** or to do harm, ...3:4
other seeds fell into **g** soil and produced grain,...........4:8
those that were sown on the **g** soil are the ones 4:20
said to Jesus, "Rabbi, it is **g** that we are here................9:5
Salt is **g**, but if the salt has lost its saltiness,............9:50
"**G** Teacher, what must I do to inherit eternal 10:17
And Jesus said to him, "Why do you call me **g**?........10:18
No one is **g** except God alone. 10:18
and whenever you want, you can do **g** for them. 14:7

GOSPEL

The beginning of the **g** of Jesus Christ,........................1:1
Jesus came into Galilee, proclaiming the **g** of 1:14
of God is at hand; repent and believe in the **g**."..........1:15
or children or lands, for my sake and for the **g**, ...10:29
the **g** must first be proclaimed to all nations.............13:10
wherever the **g** is proclaimed in the whole 14:9
and proclaim the **g** to the whole creation...................16:15

HARDNESS

with anger, grieved at their **h** of heart,........................ 3:5
"Because of your **h** of heart he wrote 10:5
for their unbelief and **h** of heart, ...16:14

HEAVEN

a voice came from **h**, "You are my beloved Son;............1:11
five loaves and the two fish he looked up to **h**........... 6:41
looking up to **h**, he sighed and said to him,...............7:34
seeking from him a sign from **h** to test him. 8:11
to the poor, and you will have treasure in **h**;.............10:21
that your Father also who is in **h** may forgive 11:25
Was the baptism of John from **h** or from man? 11:30
"If we say, 'From **h**,' he will say, 'Why then..................11:31
are given in marriage, but are like angels in **h**...........12:25
and the stars will be falling from **h**,.............................13:25
from the ends of the earth to the ends of **h**..............13:27
H and earth will pass away, but my words will...........13:31
knows, not even the angels in **h**, nor the Son,...........13:32
of Power, and coming with the clouds of **h**." 14:62
was taken up into **h** and sat down at the right..........16:19

IMMEDIATELY

i he saw the heavens being torn open.......................1:10
i drove him out into the wilderness..........................1:12

So the Son of Man is lord even of the **S**.".......................2:28
to see whether he would heal him on the **S**, ... 3:2
"Is it lawful on the **S** to do good or to do 3:4
And on the **S** he began to teach in 6:2
of Preparation, that is, the day before the **S**, ... 15:42
When the **S** was past, Mary Magdalene,...........................16:1

SATAN

the wilderness forty days, being tempted by **S**.............1:13
to them in parables, "How can **S** cast out Satan? 3:23
to them in parables, "How can Satan cast out **S**? 3:23
if **S** has risen up against himself and is divided,...........3:26
when they hear, **S** immediately comes and takes 4:15
he rebuked Peter and said, "Get behind me, **S**!...........8:33

SAVED

astonished, and said to him, "Then who can be **s**?"..10:26
But the one who endures to the end will be **s**............ 13:13
not cut short the days, no human being would be **s**.13:20
saying, "He **s** others; he cannot save himself.............. 15:31
Whoever believes and is baptized will be **s**,................16:16

SEIZED

For it was Herod who had sent and **s** John and...........6:17
And they laid hands on him and **s** him. 14:46
but a linen cloth about his body. And they **s** him,......14:51
for trembling and astonishment had **s** them,................16:8

SERVANT

be first, he must be last of all and **s** of all." 9:35
would be great among you must be your **s**,...............10:43
sent a **s** to the tenants to get from them some of.......12:2
Again he sent to them another **s**,......................................12:4
his sword and struck the **s** of the high priest.............14:47
one of the **s** girls of the high priest came,..................14:66
And the **s** girl saw him and began again to say to....14:69

SILENT

him, saying, "Be **s**, and come out of him!"......................1:25
harm, to save life or to kill?" But they were **s**.................3:4
But they kept **s**, for on the way they had.......................9:34
And many rebuked him, telling him to be **s**. 10:48
But he remained **s** and made no answer. 14:61

SINNERS

tax collectors and **s** were reclining with Jesus 2:15
that he was eating with **s** and tax collectors,................2:16
"Why does he eat with tax collectors and **s**?"..............2:16
I came not to call the righteous, but **s**." 2:17
The Son of Man is betrayed into the hands of **s**.........14:41

SORROWFUL

he went away **s**, for he had great possessions. 10:22
They began to be **s** and to say to him one 14:19
said to them, "My soul is very **s**, even to death.........14:34

SOUL

a man to gain the whole world and forfeit his **s**? 8:36
For what can a man give in return for his **s**?................8:37
your God with all your heart and with all your **s**.......12:30
to them, "My **s** is very sorrowful, even to death........14:34

TABLE

And as he reclined at **t** in his house, many tax collectors ..2:15
yet even the dogs under the **t** eat the children's.........7:28
in the house of Simon the leper, as he was reclining at **t**,..14:3
And as they were reclining at **t** and eating, ...14:18
to the eleven themselves as they were reclining at **t**,...16:14

TAUGHT

for he **t** them as one who had authority,.......................1:22
Jesus and told him all that they had done and **t**. 6:30
And again, as was his custom, he **t** them......................10:1
as Jesus **t** in the temple, he said, "How can the.........12:35

UNBELIEF

And he marveled because of their **u**. 6:6
cried out and said, "I believe; help my **u**!" 9:24
he rebuked them for their **u** and hardness of 16:14

VOICE

the **v** of one crying in the wilderness:................................1:3
a **v** came from heaven, "You are my beloved Son; 1:11
convulsing him and crying out with a loud **v**,...............1:26
with a loud **v**, he said, "What have you to do................5:7
a **v** came out of the cloud, "This is my beloved 9:7
Jesus cried with a loud **v**, "Eloi, Eloi, lema................. 15:34

WITNESS

Do not steal, Do not bear false **w**,...............................10:19
kings for my sake, to bear **w** before them.....................13:9
For many bore false **w** against him,............................14:56
stood up and bore false **w** against him, ... 14:57

WRITTEN

As it is **w** in Isaiah the prophet, ...1:2
did Isaiah prophesy of you hypocrites, as it is **w**, ...7:6
how is it **w** of the Son of Man that he should 9:12
to him whatever they pleased, as it is **w** of him." 9:13
"Is it not **w**, 'My house shall be called a house of 11:17
For the Son of Man goes as it is **w** of him, ...14:21
"You will all fall away, for it is **w**, 'I will strike............. 14:27